The New SAT® Handbook

A Tutor-Tested Review of the Skills You'll Need for Test Day and Beyond

Joy Givens, MEd, and Andrew Cole, MA

SAT® is a trademark registered and/or owned by the College Board, which was not involved in the production of, and does not endorse, this product.

SAT® is a trademark registered and/or owned by the College Board, which was not involved in the production of, and does not endorse, this product.

The New SAT Handbook: A Tutor-Tested Review of the Skills You'll Need for Test Day and Beyond

Copyright © 2016 by Joy Givens and Andrew Cole

Published by Tributaries, LLC – Pittsburgh, PA

Updated 1 Nov, 2016

All rights reserved. The text of this book, or any part thereof, may not be reproduced, stored in a retrieval system, or transmitted in any form or by any means, without the prior written permission of the publisher.

ISBN-13: 978-1-52360-345-9

Contents

Introduction 5

Chapter 1: About the New SAT 9

Chapter 2: The Reading Test 13

Chapter 3: Reading Practice Set 27

Chapter 4: The Writing and Language Test 41

Chapter 5: Grammar and Style Review 47

Chapter 6: Writing and Language Practice Set 101

Chapter 7: The Math Test 111

Chapter 8: Calculator-Free Math Drills 131

Chapter 9: Math Concepts Reference 147

Chapter 10: Math Practice Set 209

Chapter 11: The Essay Test 217

Chapter 12: Essay Practice Prompts 235

Chapter 13: The Final Word 243

Index 249

Notes Pages 252

Introduction

We've all had that nightmare: you wake up panicked, realizing that you have overslept and are now late for the *all-important test*. You race to school in a blur, throw yourself into your desk, stare down at the test, and realize that you don't recognize a word on it. And you crammed all night for this. And you're not wearing anything.

When you wake up from this nightmare—because hopefully this hasn't actually happened to you—you might calm yourself down by saying something along the lines of, "It's okay, I've still got x weeks/months before the test. There's still plenty of time to study."

While this is often true, it's remarkable how suddenly "There's still plenty of time" can turn into "Oh, that's *this* week?!" It's hard enough to find the time to study for tests and write papers for your classes. How are you supposed to study for a marathon test like the SAT?

You cannot cram for the SAT. It is an almost-four-hour test comprised of dozens of multiple-choice questions, an optional essay, and topics ranging from geometric probability to inferential reading. It is massive, it gives you writer's cramp and brain ache, and it is designed to test what you have learned over a period of years. Nobody can cram for that.

Now, before you feel the need to hurl this book (or yourself) out the closest window, look for the silver lining in studying for this uncrammable test: though you can't successfully cram for the SAT, you *can* successfully plan for it.

Planning ahead for the SAT allows you to work with small, manageable pieces of information. When you can review for half an hour during study hall or while you're waiting for the bus, you don't need to set aside twelve hours each weekend. (Good grief, please don't do that to yourself.)

Planning ahead means that, rather than freak out about the SAT as a whole, you can practice one concrete, achievable skill at a time. It's like defeating Godzilla with a series of strategic paper cuts.

Studying for the SAT in this way will help you not only to achieve your best score but also to prepare for college in and of itself. Think about it:

- You have a long-term goal with a deadline: test day.
- The study materials are all available to you in advance.
- The assignments are largely self-guided, and only the final grade matters.

In writing this book, we recognize that you, a busy high school student, have little time to spare, so we've avoided making one of those bloated thousand-page books. Everything that you need to know is in here, but nothing else. Think of this book as an organic, local, free-range, grain-fed new SAT guide, with no artificial flavors or fillers (except for the occasional quirky metaphor).

This book, though it does include several chapters of practice problems for each content area, does not contain full-length practice tests. We don't have test-writing elves in our closets, unfortunately.

However, with excellent, often free practice available from the test makers (www.collegeboard.org), you can easily access hundreds of genuine SAT problems online and use this guide as a handy reference and identifier of what you want to review the most.

Here are three more useful things about this book:

- We know that each student has different strengths, so the chapters have been clearly indexed and organized so that you can zero in on the topics you personally need to study.

- We recognize that your first priority is to be a successful high school student. That's why many of the strategies and concepts in this book can be applied not just to the SAT but also to coursework in high school *and* college.

- We also understand that you're probably not super-excited to spend your precious free time preparing for a standardized test, so we've tried to make it as engaging (and occasionally even entertaining) as possible. Keep an eye out for helpful tips from our kitschy little mascot, Cecil the Pencil, while you read!

"Hey there, scholar! I'm Cecil the Pencil. I'll pop up occasionally to offer you my Tips to Stay Sharp* throughout the SAT."

*Get it? The pencil has "Tips to Stay Sharp!" Nothing like a few puns to keep you moving as you study, right?

Now, before you read any further, take a moment to set this book down on your coffee table or desk or wherever you're reading and please do one thing for us.

Tell yourself that you are smart.

Go ahead, say it out loud: "I am smart, and I can handle this test."

Every student has unique strengths and weaknesses, and you'll identify yours as you study. But we are *so* over students saying things like "I'm just terrible at math," "I can't understand the readings," "I've never been a good writer," and so on. So before you dive headlong into your SAT preparations, remind yourself that you are smart, and you can handle this test. You're already making a smart decision by planning ahead.

Thanks for choosing this guide to help you prepare. **Good luck!**

8

Chapter 1: About the New SAT

The new SAT is a 3-hour test (not including the optional 50-minute Essay Test) that includes four multiple-choice sections in Math, Reading, and Writing and Language. Here is the order of the test sections:

> ***Reading Test*** – 65 minutes, 52 multiple-choice questions
>
> ***Writing and Language Test*** – 35 minutes, 44 multiple-choice questions
>
> ***Math Test*** (no calculator) – 25 minutes, 20 multiple-choice and grid-in questions
>
> ***Math Test*** (calculator) – 55 minutes, 38 multiple-choice and grid-in questions
>
> ***Essay Test*** (optional) – 50 minutes, one essay prompt

What topics are tested?

The ***Reading Test*** assesses your reading comprehension and critical thinking skills. You will be given four single passages and one set of paired passages. Similar to the previous format of the SAT, the questions will require that you carefully analyze the provided texts without personal interpretation.

Unlike the former SAT, the Reading Test of the new SAT does not include fill-in-the-blank vocabulary questions. For detailed information about the Reading Test, refer to Chapter 2, beginning on page 13.

The *Writing and Language Test* assesses your knowledge of Standard English grammar and style, error correction, and overall composition. You will be provided with four passages, each of which will contain grammatical, stylistic, and/or compositional errors. Most of the multiple-choice questions will ask you to correct an underlined word or phrase if necessary, and the remainder will ask you about the logic or structure of a passage. For detailed information about the Writing and Language Test, refer to Chapter 4, beginning on page 41.

The *Math Test* assesses your mathematical and critical thinking skills in the following College Board-identified target areas: "Heart of Algebra," "Problem Solving and Data Analysis," "Passport to Advanced Math," and "Additional Topics in Math." 45 of the questions will be multiple-choice, and the other 13 will be student-produced response (grid-in) questions.

Unlike the former SAT, the Math Test of the new SAT is split into two sections, the first of which must be completed with no calculator. The no-calculator test will not include Problem Solving and Data Analysis questions. For detailed information about the Math Test, refer to Chapter 7, beginning on page 111.

The *Essay Test* assesses your ability to analyze a source document (in this case, a persuasive text intended for a large audience) and write an essay that evaluates the argument and evidence given by the source. No outside knowledge is required for the essay, but you will need to demonstrate strong composition skills as you organize and express your ideas on the passage, using evidence from the text to support your own argument. For more detailed information on the Essay Test, refer to Chapter 11, beginning on page 217.

How is the new SAT scored?

The new SAT calculates and reports a whole lot of scores: subscores, test scores, cross-test scores, area scores, and a composite score. Whew! We'll quickly define each of them for you, but if you want more information about how the various new SAT scores are calculated and used, visit the test makers' official website: www.collegeboard.org.

> *Subscores*: The Reading, Writing and Language, and Math tests will have topical subscores scaled from 1 to 15, based on the question content types. The Essay Test will receive subscores between 2 and 8 for three key components: Reading, Analysis, and Writing.
>
> *Test scores*: The Reading, Writing and Language, and Math tests will be scaled into scores ranging from 10 to 40.

Cross-test scores: Questions on specific topics from the Reading, Writing and Language, and Math tests will be used to calculate "Analysis in History/Social Studies" and "Analysis in Science" scores, ranging from 10 to 40.

Area scores: The Reading Test and the Writing and Language Test will be combined and scaled to create the Evidence-Based Reading and Writing area score, and both sections of the Math Test will be combined and scaled to create the Math area score. Both area scores will range from 200 to 800.

Composite Score: Your Evidence-Based Reading and Writing area score and your Math area score will be combined into your composite score, ranging from 400 to 1600.

It's also important to note that, unlike the previous SAT, the new SAT will have ***no wrong-answer penalty***. That means that you should not leave any questions blank—there's no harm in giving a question your best guess, even if you are unsure of that question or running out of time.

Ideally, however, you will feel prepared enough to answer any question the new SAT can throw at you. For all the strategies, content review, and information you'll need to feel completely ready, read on!

Chapter 2: The Reading Test

Overview

The Reading Test measures your ability to read and understand several passages of text and then to answer questions about those passages. Sounds simple enough, right?

It is! However, both the passages and their questions are designed to test your abilities to spot key details and draw inferences. Even though its structure is simple, the Reading Test's content is often complex, so read on for plenty of details, tips, and strategies to help you do well on this section.

How will the test be set up?

You'll be given four single passages and one set of paired passages. The passages will be roughly 500 to 750 words each, and the paired passages will be shorter than the single ones. Some of the passages may include graphs or other visual data, and you'll be asked about those as well.

All the passages will be excerpts from articles, books, or other published sources, rather than passages written specifically for the SAT. Some passages may be narrative, some may be informational, and some may be persuasive. The passages will cover a range of topics, including science, social studies and history, and U.S. and world literature.

Each of the single passages and the set of paired passages will be followed by ten or eleven questions, for 52 questions total. You'll have 65 minutes for this part of the test.

Will I have to know anything about the subject in order to answer the questions?

Cecil's Tips to Stay Sharp

Even with Vocabulary in Context questions, you will have enough information within the passage to find the right answer, whether you recognize the words or not.

No. Outside knowledge might help you to settle in as you read, but this section of the test is about how well you can read and understand the passage at hand. Everything that you will need to know to answer the questions can be found in the passage.

If the passage has an introduction, it's a good idea to read that introduction. You won't be asked about the introduction directly, but it can provide supplementary information that might help you answer some questions about the passage.

In other words, don't worry about cramming for history, science, or literature or memorizing long vocabulary lists. The best way to prepare for this part of the test is to build your skills of analysis and interpretation. And as you build those skills through breaking down complex passages, your vocabulary skills will improve as well.

Question Types

The questions will come in three basic types: Analysis of the Topic, Command of Evidence, and Vocabulary in Context. The question types won't be labeled on the test, but you'll probably be able to tell what kind of question you're being asked anyway.

Analysis of the Topic questions

These questions cover a few different skills, but in one way or another they're all about how to understand the passage and its various parts. They might cover things like:

- the main ideas or themes of the text
- the relationships between ideas in the text

- the arguments and evidence the author uses in the text
- the overall structure, tone, or mood of the text
- the author's purpose or point of view in writing the text
- the meaning and use of statistics, graphs, or other quantitative information
- the relationships between the paired passages or parts of the paired passages

That's not necessarily a complete list, but you get the idea. Analysis of the Topic questions will take different forms, but essentially they'll ask what the passage says and what it means.

Command of Evidence questions

These questions are all about how evidence from the passage supports your interpretations of things in the passage. They'll be asking what makes you think your interpretations are right, in other words. Command of Evidence questions are usually easy to spot, because they often take a form like, "Which choice provides the best evidence for your answer to the previous question?"

Of course, it helps if your answer to the previous question was correct to begin with, so make sure you're basing *all* your answers on the passage.

Vocabulary in Context questions

You can probably guess that these questions will ask you what a given word or phrase means or how it is used in the passage. For the most part, the SAT won't be asking about obscure or esoteric words or about the technical jargon of a particular field of study; it also won't be asking you to define words out of thin air. Instead, usually it will pick a word that has multiple meanings and ask what that word means in *that* specific instance. Even if you don't recognize the word, you'll probably have enough clues from the context to figure out the answer.

Vocabulary in Context questions look like this: "As used in line 16, *garnish* most nearly means…" The answer choices will give definitions of the word, and in this case they might include things like "to deduct money owed from the debtor's wages" and "to adorn, as with parsley." You need to pick the definition that best fits the context of the passage.

How to get through the passages

A lot of people assume that it's enough just to read the passage the same way you'd read anything else, but that's not the best way to approach these SAT reading passages.

Obviously, you need to *read* the passage, and also the brief introductory text that comes with it, which can give you some clues about what the passage is about and help you focus your reading a little better. But the kind of reading that will help you most is not passive reading, running your eyes over the words as fast as you can and hoping that enough of them stick in your brain to let you answer the questions. You need to read *actively*.

What does it mean to "read actively"? It means that you participate in the process of figuring out for yourself what the text means, rather than just sit back and wait for the author to explain it for you. It means that you take note of not only what a passage says, but also *why* and *how* it says it. If you read the passage actively, you'll understand it much better and be able to answer the questions about it much more easily.

Reading actively

Read the passage with your pencil in your hand. As you read, underline things you think are important. Draw circles around things, draw asterisks next to things, draw arrows connecting things. Write notes in the margins. Any notes or marks that will help you understand the passage better belong right on the page where you can use them.

Remember, you can write in your test booklet all you want. It'll get destroyed after you're through with it, so you don't have to worry about leaving the pages clean for anyone else. And you're not graded based on what you write in your test booklet; only what you mark on your answer sheet counts.

What you write or mark or underline is up to you. Anything that helps you to understand the passage better is fair game. But here are a few suggestions:

- Next to each paragraph, jot down the main idea of that paragraph in a few words or a key phrase. This helps you slow down just enough to take it in better.

- Use your own shorthand. For example, write the Greek letter theta (θ) in the margin next to the passage's thesis or main idea and put an X next to each example.

- Underline important ideas or arguments.

- Circle words or phrases that show an emotion or indicate the tone of the passage.
- Draw arrows connecting parts of the passage that show cause and effect, similarity, or contrast.

Don't let your active reading take up *too* much time, since answering the questions is what counts. But you'll find that the extra minute or two you spend on reading actively will save you a lot of time later on, because you won't need to keep re-reading the passage to find what you need to answer the questions.

Incidentally, active reading is a great skill for life, not just for the SAT. Use it in your classes and on your homework, use it throughout high school and college, use it in your professional life, and use it any time you really want to understand what you're reading!

In fact, we're such big fans of active reading that we're going to give you a passage to practice on right now! Here you go:

Cecil's Tips to Stay Sharp

*If you're not sure what to include in your notes, just remember the word **NOTE**: **N**arrative (author's tone and voice), **O**pinions (the author's and others'), **T**hesis (or main idea), and **E**vidence (examples, reasoning, etc).*

Active-Reading Practice Passage

Born in Canada and educated in England, Grant Allen became known for both his novels and short stories, and his perceptive studies of natural science. In this excerpt from his 1889 essay "Falling in Love," Allen responds to a social reformer's idea that the human race would benefit if experts selected people's spouses for them in order to propagate desirable genetic traits through their descendants.

Falling in Love, as modern biology teaches us to believe, is nothing more than the latest, highest, and most involved exemplification, in the human [5] race, of that almost universal selective process which Mr. Darwin has enabled us to recognise throughout the whole long series of the animal kingdom. The butterfly that circles and eddies in his [10] aërial dance around his observant mate is endeavouring to charm her by the delicacy of his colouring, and to overcome her coyness by the display of his skill. The peacock that struts about in impe- [15] rial pride under the eyes of his attentive hens, is really contributing to the future beauty and strength of his race. …

In our own species, the selective pro- [20] cess is marked by all the features common to selection throughout the whole animal kingdom; but it is also, as might be expected, far more specialised, far more individualised, far more cognisant of personal traits and minor peculiarities. It is further-more exerted to a far greater extent upon mental and moral as well as physical peculiarities in the individual. ...

I have spoken throughout, for argument's sake, as though the only interest to be considered in the married relation were the interests of the offspring, and so ultimately of the race at large, rather than of the persons themselves who enter into it. But I do not quite see why each generation should thus be sacrificed to the welfare of the generations that afterwards succeed it. Now it is one of the strongest points in favour of the system of falling in love that it does, by common experience in the vast majority of instances, assort together persons who subsequently prove themselves thoroughly congenial and helpful to one another. And this result I look upon as one great proof of the real value and importance of the instinct. Most men and women select for themselves partners for life at an age when they know but little of the world, when they judge but superficially of characters and motives, when they still make many mistakes in the conduct of life and in the estimation of chances. Yet most of them find in after days that they have really chosen out of all the world one of the persons best adapted by native idiosyncrasy to make their joint lives enjoyable and useful.

I make every allowance for the effects of habit, for the growth of sentiment, for the gradual approximation of tastes and sympathies; but surely, even so, it is a common consciousness with every one of us who has been long married, that we could hardly conceivably have made ourselves happy with any of the partners whom others have chosen; and that we have actually made ourselves so with the partners we chose for ourselves under the guidance of an almost unerring native instinct. ...

Remember, there's no one "right" way to read actively; the whole point is to help *you* understand the passage. If your notes help you understand it better, then you did it right!

To help you check your understanding of the passage, though, here are some example notes on the thesis and main ideas of the passage:

Thesis: "Now it is one of... and importance of the instinct." (Lines 39-48. Notice how the thesis isn't always at the beginning of a passage, and it isn't always confined to one sentence.) In other words, "Falling in love usually puts together good partners; that's why it's important."

Main Idea of Paragraph 1: Animals choose mates based on physical qualities—good for species.

Main Idea of Paragraph 2: Humans choose mates based on physical, mental, *and* moral qualities.

Main Idea of Paragraph 3: Falling in love instinct usually matches good mates who improve each other's lives.

Main Idea of Paragraph 4: Long-married humans see love as a kind of native instinct.

You probably noted ideas similar to these in the passage, but if you described them differently, that's just fine. Like we said, the point of active reading is to help *you* understand the passage. If you understand the passage, you're doing it right.

Look back over the passage. What other details did you see that support the main ideas? What else did you underline or mark? What notes did you jot in the margins? Can you see how Allen used these ideas, details, and other elements to construct his main argument?

And that's active reading—a process that helps you identify main ideas and supporting details, see how a passage is put together, and understand an author's argument. Not really so scary, is it?

Should I read the questions before I read the passage?

It might seem logical to read the questions first so you know what to look for when you're reading the passage. That way, as you read, you can zero in on specific words and other parts of the passage that apply to the questions you'll actually have to answer, right?

But we recommend *not* reading the questions beforehand—for precisely that reason.

If you read the questions beforehand, you'll prime your brain to spot those key words and phrases in the passage. Your brain will scan for those words and phrases; when it sees one, it'll check it off a list, then move on to scan for the next one. It will basically have the opposite effect of active reading—you will know where things are in the passage, but not what they mean or how they are connected.

This is especially true for questions about overall tone or purpose, or the ones that use phrases like "most important." For those questions you need to have a good sense of the passage as a whole, and you won't have one if all your brain was doing was scanning for key words.

Instead, read the passage first, *then* read the questions. You can always look back to the passage while working through the questions, but it will be easier if you already know where to look for what you need.

How should I handle the paired passages?

The paired passages are two shorter passages written on the same topic or theme by different authors. They allow you to analyze and evaluate different perspectives on the same broad theme or issue. You'll get a few questions about each passage by itself and a few questions that ask you to relate the passages to each other.

Read the paired passages actively, the same way you'd read the single passages. But since you're dealing with two passages here, you should also look for ways the passages relate to each other. You might find things like:

- points on which the authors agree or disagree

- different angles from which the authors approach the same theme or issue

- different interpretations the authors give for the same evidence

- different strategies the authors use to argue their points

- similarities or differences in the authors' purposes, intended audiences, or tones

These things can play out in all kinds of ways. For example, maybe one author is optimistic about scientific advances while the other is more skeptical. Maybe one author is trying to persuade Congress to pass a certain law while the other is trying to persuade the general public to oppose it. Maybe one author relies on emotions to persuade his or her audience while the other uses statistics—or maybe they both use the same statistics, but one thinks that those statistics are reliable while the other does not. Or maybe …

Well, you get the idea.

Don't worry about trying to identify every single similarity or difference as you read. You'll only be asked a handful of questions about both passages. But these are some of the things you might be asked about, so they're worth keeping an eye out for.

What if I don't understand the passage or just can't get through it?

The College Board isn't trying to trick you into looking foolish by giving you a difficult passage full of land mines. They're also not trying to make you angry or put you to sleep. But you might end up with a passage you have trouble with or one you just don't like. Sometimes it happens.

If you don't understand the passage

If you've read through a passage and you didn't understand it, review your notes. Go back to the basics. Can you identify the main idea? Can you identify some of the reasons, examples, or details the author provides to support the main idea? Can you identify the author's mood, or at least whether it's mainly positive or negative?

If going back over the passage with your notes helps, great! Now move on to the questions!

But if reviewing it doesn't help, try reading a couple of the questions to see if those help you understand the passage better. Remember, though, this should *not* be your starting point for every passage! As we said above, it is best to understand the passage first. But if the passage is giving you a lot of trouble, it can occasionally be a good fall-back to try out a *couple* of questions. And since the questions are multiple-choice, one of the answers has to be right. If you see a question about the main idea, for example, you can compare it to the passage and eliminate answers that don't fit or make sense. Even if you don't totally understand everything in the passage, reading actively will help you to know what's *not* in the passage.

If you don't agree with the passage

You might see a passage in which the author says something you don't agree with, something that seems incorrect, or maybe even something you think is appalling. The College Board isn't aiming to stir up controversy, but it also can't predict the views of every single student.

Unfortunately, you can't skip a passage. What you can do is adjust your approach to it.

The world is full of people who have different views on a wide variety of subjects, and you'll only be able to change people's minds by listening to them, trying to see things from their point of view, and engaging in dialogue with them. So think of that SAT reading passage as an opportunity to practice the first two of those three things.

Even if you disagree with the author, try to understand what he or she is really saying and how and why he or she is saying it; after all, that's what most of the questions are getting at, in one way or another. If it helps, you can even imagine that you want to have a dialogue with the author so you can try to change his or her mind.

And if all else fails, keep in mind that the better you understand someone else's argument, the more effectively you'll be able to dismantle it.

If the passage is boring

You may get lucky and get an SAT test booklet full of fascinating, well written passages. If so, wonderful! But you may also wind up with a passage that's really dull. Puts-you-to-sleep dull. What then?

The sad truth is that sometimes in life you'll have to read boring stuff that's important for you to read anyway. Maybe you've already encountered readings like that in high school, and you'll probably encounter some in college and in jobs later on. It may help you to think of a boring SAT passage as practice for helping you extract valuable knowledge from dull texts later in life.

Fortunately, as mentioned above, the College Board chooses SAT reading passages from a variety of subject areas and kinds of writing. Even if you find one passage boring, the next one might be more interesting. Reading actively works just as well on a boring passage as it does on an interesting one!

Take your active reading back to the basics: thesis or main idea, examples or evidence, opinions, and author mood or voice. Carefully pick out those key elements like you'd pick your favorite candy out of a big bowl, use them to answer the questions as best you can, and move on.

How to Handle the Questions

Here's the short version: If you know the answer to the question, go right ahead and find the answer choice that you know is right. If you don't know it off the top of your head, go back to the passage and use it and your notes to help you find the answer. Then pick the answer choice that best matches what you found in the passage.

Now here's a more detailed look at how to answer the different types of questions you might see:

Analysis of the Topic questions

Analysis of the Topic questions are basically asking what the passage says and what it means. As we noted above, they can include questions about the passage's tone, purpose, main idea, arguments, structure, audience, or any of several other elements.

Some Analysis of the Topic questions will refer you to specific lines, paragraphs, examples, or other parts of the passage. To answer these questions, you should *always* go back and read the part of the passage mentioned in the question. Look at the parts immediately before and after it as well, and consider how it fits into the passage as a whole. Extra context will often help you.

Other Analysis of the Topic questions will ask you about the passage in general without identifying a specific part of the passage for you to review. Maybe you have a good enough sense of the passage to be able to answer the question right away, but it's always a good idea to go back to the passage to make sure you've understood it correctly. The notes you took while reading the passage can help you find the most relevant parts of the passage more easily.

Command of the Evidence questions

Command of the Evidence questions ask you to identify the sentence, example, or other element from the passage that provides the best evidence for the answer you gave to the previous question. In other words, they're not asking you how the author uses evidence—they're asking how *you* use evidence.

That's a good thing, actually. Command of the Evidence questions force you to think about how effectively you're basing your analysis on actual evidence from the passage. And that means they can give you great practice and help you to build great habits. Basing your arguments on evidence is a skill you'll need throughout college and your professional life.

Maybe one of the answer choices for a Command of the Evidence question will be exactly the piece of evidence you used yourself. If so, great! Check the other choices anyway to see whether there's an even better one, but chances are good that you're on the right track.

But maybe you don't see the evidence you used among the answer choices for the Command of the Evidence question you're now faced with. If this happens, don't panic. You'll want to do two things:

> First, look over the answer choices for the Command of the Evidence question and see whether any of them makes sense as evidence for your answer to the previous question. Even if you used different evidence, one of the choices you're now being offered might still be good evidence for your answer.
>
> Second, go back to the previous question and double-check your answer. If none

of the choices in the Command of the Evidence question fits the answer you gave for the previous question, then maybe a different answer would fit the available evidence better.

Vocabulary in Context questions

The Vocabulary in Context questions *seem* simple enough. After all, they're just asking what certain words mean, right? But they're often trickier than they look.

As we mentioned above, a lot of the words you'll see in the Vocabulary in Context questions have more than one meaning. These questions aren't just asking you for any definition that fits the word—they're asking you what a word means *in a particular part of a passage*. And the only way to be sure is to go back to that part of the passage.

Sometimes reading the sentence in which the word appears will give you enough context. In those cases, treat the word in question like a blank; as you read the sentence, fill in another word that makes sense to you (don't worry about what the answer choices say). *Then* go to the answer choices and find the best match. If there's not enough context for you to assess the word in that one sentence, then start a sentence earlier and reread until you get through the sentence after the one in question. That will give you greater context to define the word.

If I'm having trouble with a question, should I skip it and come back later?

If you have trouble answering a question right away, it's tempting to circle it in your test booklet, move on, and come back to it later. But we don't exactly recommend doing that with the Reading Test, and here's why:

The questions on the SAT Reading Test are all based on particular passages. You'll have a passage, then some questions about that passage, then another passage, then some questions about *that* passage, and so on. Therefore, the best way to keep your focus is to answer all the questions for one passage, then move on to the questions for the next passage. If you skip around among passages, it'll be too easy for you to mix up important details.

That being said, you can certainly answer the questions in any order you like, so consider this course of action: if a question on the Reading Test gives you trouble, circle it, skip it, and answer the rest of the questions for that passage. Then come back to the one you skipped while that passage is still fresh in your mind. The process of answering the other questions will likely help you to figure out the one you had trouble with.

If you revisit a question and you're still stuck, then move on to the other reading passages and come back to it again later if you have time. Remember, there is no wrong answer penalty on the new SAT, so you shouldn't leave anything blank!

Making Inferences, Not Assumptions

Now that you have reviewed how to approach the passages and the questions, there's one more key concept to review: the difference between an assumption and an inference. Analysis of the Topic questions that ask what the author "would most likely" say or do, for example, or questions that ask you to draw a conclusion based on the facts of the passage, are questions that require you to make ***inferences***.

The tricky thing about making inferences is that they often can get mixed up with assumptions. Let's start by defining the two terms:

> An ***inference*** is a conclusion based upon evidence (meaning facts and logical reasoning). On the new SAT, the evidence that you need will always be found within the passage.

> An ***assumption*** is a conclusion that may or may not be correct, because it is lacking in evidence. On the new SAT, assumptions will appear often in the answer choices, but they will not be supported by evidence from the passage.

Here's an example of inferences versus assumptions. Suppose it's about nine o'clock one night in January. You stayed indoors all afternoon and evening, and you suddenly get a text message from a friend down the block that reads, "OMG have u looked outside? It snowed a foot in the last 6 hrs!" Of the following four statements, which is an ***inference*** you could make?

(A) Woo-hoo! Snow day tomorrow for sure!
(B) Yikes, it will snow another six inches by midnight!
(C) I better finish up my homework before the snow knocks out our power like it did last time.
(D) Glad I stayed inside. It must have been freezing out there this afternoon.

Let's talk these through. (A) sounds reasonable—a foot of snow probably would lead to a snow day the next day. However, what if the day in question is a Friday or Saturday? Or what if you are home-schooled? Or what if your town has really speedy snowplows so that the schools never have snow days? There is just not enough evidence given to support (A), so it is an *assumption*.

Next, there's (B), which looks like a clever application of the rate given in the problem: 12 inches in 6 hours means 2 inches per hour... so there would be 6 more inches after another 3 hours. However, you would be making an *assumption* that the snow will continue to fall constantly at the same rate.

(C) is also convincing, especially since finishing your homework in case the power goes out would be such a prudent choice. If the snow knocked out your electricity last time, isn't it reasonable to infer that it would happen again? The short answer is no. One occurrence does not a pattern make. If the snow always knocked out your power without fail, then you could make this conclusion. Since it only happened once, it's an *assumption*.

(D) is a reasonable conclusion that can be made based on what we know about snow—namely, that it must be 32 degrees Fahrenheit or below for snow to fall and accumulate. Since there is evidence to support this conclusion, it is an *inference*.

You need to be just as stringent when making inferences and choosing your answers on the Reading Test, because every word counts. It is always worth taking the time to make sure that the answers you choose are backed up by what the passage says or implies. Go back to the passage!

A Final Note

You may have noticed this already, but we want to point out here that there's a common thread in the strategies for answering the different question types: Go back to the passage.

That's because the best way to find the answer to *any* question in the SAT Reading Test is to go back to the passage. It is literally an open-book test. You can find the answers to all the questions by going back to the passage. Use your notes and underlinings and markings to help you, but in any case…

Go back to the passage.

Chapter 3: Reading Practice Set

On the next few pages are some sample passages and question sets that resemble the ones you'll see on the test. Practice actively reading the passages and use your notes to work through the questions. If you're reading an electronic version of this study guide, use a piece of scratch paper to keep track of your notes, or print a copy of the pages if possible. Enjoy!

Practice Passage One: A Regular Passage

Florence Nightingale first came to prominence nursing sick and wounded English soldiers in the Crimean War, then went on to become the founder of modern nursing and an advocate for sanitary reform. This excerpt from her 1861 book Directions for Cooking by Troops, in Camp and Hospital *details her recommendations for how and when to feed weak patients.*

Every careful observer of the sick will agree in this, that thousands of patients are annually starved in the midst of plenty, from want of attention
5 to the ways which alone make it possible for them to take food. This want of attention is as remarkable in those who urge upon the sick to do what is quite impossible to them, as in
10 the sick themselves who will not make the effort to do what is perfectly possible to them.

For instance, to the large majority of very weak patients it is quite
15 impossible to take any solid food before 11 A. M., nor then, if their strength is still further exhausted by fasting till that hour. For weak patients have generally feverish nights, and, in
20 the morning, dry mouths; and, if they could eat with those dry mouths, it would be the worse for them. A

spoonful of beef-tea[1], of arrowroot and wine[2], of egg flip[3], every hour, will give them the requisite nourishment, and prevent them from being too much exhausted to take at a later hour the solid food, which is necessary for their recovery. And every patient who can swallow at all can swallow these liquid things, if he chooses. But how often do we hear a mutton-chop, an egg, a bit of bacon, ordered to a patient for breakfast, to whom (as a moment's consideration would show us) it must be quite impossible to masticate such things at that hour.

Again, a nurse is ordered to give a patient a tea-cup full of some article of food every three hours. The patient's stomach rejects it. If so, try a table-spoonfull every hour; if this will not do, a tea-spoonfull every quarter of an hour.

I am bound to say, that I think more patients are lost by want of care and ingenuity in these momentous minutiæ in private nursing than in public hospitals. And I think there is more of the *entente cordiale*[4] to assist one another's hands between the Doctor and his head Nurse in the latter institutions, than between the doctor and the patient's friends in the private house.

If we did but know the consequences which may ensue, in very weak patients, from ten minutes' fasting or repletion (I call it repletion when they are obliged to let too small an interval elapse between taking food and some other exertion, owing to the nurse's unpunctuality), we should be more careful never to let this occur. In very weak patients there is often a nervous difficulty of swallowing, which is so much increased by any other call upon their strength that, unless they have their food punctually at the minute, which minute again must be arranged so as to fall in with no other minute's occupation, they can take nothing till the next respite occurs—so that an unpunctuality or delay of ten minutes may very well turn out to be one of two or three hours. And why is it not as easy to be punctual to a minute? Life often literally hangs upon these minutes.

In acute cases, where life or death is to be determined in a few hours, these matters are very generally attended to, especially in Hospitals; and the number of cases is large where the patient is, as it were, brought back to life by exceeding care on the part of the Doctor or Nurse, or both, in ordering and giving nourishment with minute selection and punctuality.

But in chronic cases, lasting over months and years, where the fatal issue is often determined at last by mere protracted starvation, I had rather not enumerate the instances which I have known where a little ingenuity, and a great deal of perseverance, might, in all probability, have averted the result. The consulting the hours when the patient can take food, the observation of the times, often varying, when he is most faint, the altering seasons of taking food, in order to anticipate and prevent such times—all this, which requires observation, ingenuity, and perseverance (and these really constitute the good Nurse), might save more lives than we wot of.

---

1 A beef broth served to weak patients in need of easily digestible nutrition.
2 An easy-to-swallow mixture in which the arrowroot was thought to provide dietary starch.
3 A beverage made with egg and a spirit such as rum, given primarily as a source of protein.
4 "Cordial understanding," in this case a mutual agreement to work together for the patient's health.

Questions #1-10 are based on the previous passage.

1. The central idea of the passage is that
   (A) patients do better in hospitals than at home.
   (B) careful attention to times and methods of feeding is critical in patient care.
   (C) certain foods are better than others for the very ill.
   (D) nurses are as important as doctors when caring for the sick.

2. Which choice provides the best evidence for the answer to the previous question?
   (A) Lines 6-12 ("This want of … impossible to them")
   (B) Lines 18-22 ("For weak patients … worse for them.")
   (C) Lines 77-79 ("Life often … these minutes.")
   (D) Lines 98-108 ("The consulting … we wot of.")

3. As used in line 4, *want* most nearly means
   (A) desire.
   (B) craving.
   (C) lack.
   (D) poverty.

4. Which of the following is Nightingale's most likely reason for using the phrase "momentous minutiae" in line 47?
   (A) To highlight the large impact that small matters can have.
   (B) To indict private nurses for their inferior skills.
   (C) To appeal to doctors by using technical-sounding words.
   (D) "Momentous minutiae" was a common medicine in the 1800s.

5. Which argument would Nightingale most likely use to support her claim in lines 45-55 that faulty care in the "momentous minutiae" causes more patients to die at home than in hospitals?
   (A) Hospitals have better equipment and medicine than those available in private homes.
   (B) Hospitals are cleaner than homes, so there is less risk of infection.
   (C) Government-supported hospitals are better funded than private homes.
   (D) Trained nurses can observe and understand the details of care better than unskilled friends.

6. As used in line 92, *issue* most nearly means
   (A) matter.
   (B) flowing substance.
   (C) edition.
   (D) outcome.

7. Why does Nightingale argue that patients must "have their food punctually at the minute" (line 69)?
   (A) Patients who wait too long or not long enough may be too weak to swallow.
   (B) Busy nurses have many patients to feed and must give them all equal time.
   (C) She believes that patients recover best if schedules are imposed upon them.
   (D) Intensive treatment regimens leave patients little time to eat.

8. Which choice provides the best evidence for the answer to the previous question?
   (A) Lines 31-37 ("But how often … at that hour.")
   (B) Lines 64-76 ("In very weak … or three hours.")
   (C) Lines 13-18 ("to the large … to that hour.")
   (D) Lines 83-89 ("and the number … selection and punctuality.")

9. Nightingale would most likely argue that nurses should
   (A) feed their patients according to detailed, rigid schedules.
   (B) give all their patients small, frequent doses of liquid nourishment.
   (C) observe their patients' needs and adapt their feeding accordingly.
   (D) work in hospitals rather than in private homes or other settings.

10. It can be reasonably inferred from the passage that
    (A) more people use hospitals than at-home physician care as a result of Nightingale's book.
    (B) nurses who follow Nightingale's recommendations pay close attention to their patients' strength.
    (C) special cookbooks focused on the sick were a cottage industry in the mid-1800s.
    (D) Nightingale would go on to establish certification programs for nurses in cities around the world.

Practice Passage Two: A Set of Paired Passages

Both of the following passages describe scenes of children at Christmas. In Passage 1, from Fyodor Dostoevsky's short story "A Christmas Tree and a Wedding," the narrator recalls a party attended by children from a variety of social classes. In Passage 2, from Charles Dickens' novella A Christmas Carol, *miserly businessman Ebenezer Scrooge is shown a vision of his former sweetheart at home with her family one Christmas a few years in the past.*

Passage 1

The children were all incredibly sweet, and resolutely refused to model themselves on the "grown-ups," regardless of all the admonitions of their governesses and mammas. They stripped the Christmas tree to the last sweetmeat in the twinkling of an eye, and had succeeded in breaking half the playthings before they knew what was destined for which.

Particularly charming was a black-eyed, curly-headed boy, who kept trying to shoot me with his wooden gun. But my attention was still more attracted by his sister, a girl of eleven, quiet, dreamy, pale, with big, prominent, dreamy eyes, exquisite as a little Cupid. The children hurt her feelings in some way, and so she came away from them to the same empty parlour in which I was sitting, and played with her doll in the corner. The visitors respectfully pointed out her father, a wealthy contractor, and someone whispered that three hundred thousand roubles were already set aside for her dowry.

I turned round to glance at the group who were interested in such a circumstance, and my eye fell on Yulian Mastakovitch, who, with his hands behind his back and his head on one side, was listening with the greatest attention to these gentlemen's idle gossip. Afterwards I could not help admiring the discrimination of the host and hostess in the distribution of the children's presents. The little girl, who had already a portion of three hundred thousand roubles, received the costliest doll. Then followed presents diminishing in value in accordance with the rank of the parents of these happy children; finally, the child of lowest degree, a thin, freckled, red-haired little boy of ten, got nothing but a book of stories about the marvels of nature and tears of devotion, etc., without pictures or even woodcuts. He was the son of a poor widow, the governess of the children of the house, an oppressed and scared little boy. He was dressed in a short jacket of inferior nankin[5]. After receiving his book he walked round the other toys for a long time; he longed to play with the other children, but did not dare; it was evident that he already felt and understood his position.

I love watching children. Their first independent approaches to life are extremely interesting. I noticed that the red-haired boy was so fascinated by the costly toys of the other children, especially by a theatre in which he certainly longed to take some part, that he made up his mind to sacrifice his dignity. He smiled and began playing with the other children, he gave away his apple to a fat-faced little boy who had a mass of goodies tied up in a pocket-handkerchief already, and even brought himself to carry another

---

[5] A durable yellow or buff-colored cotton fabric, also sometimes spelled "nankeen."

boy on his back, simply not to be turned away from the theatre, but an insolent youth gave him a heavy thump a minute later. The child did not dare to cry. Then the governess, his mother, made her appearance, and told him not to interfere with the other children's playing. The boy went away to the same room in which was the little girl. She let him join her, and the two set to work very eagerly dressing the expensive doll.

Passage 2

They[6] were in another scene and place; a room, not very large or handsome, but full of comfort. Near to the winter fire sat a beautiful young girl, so like that last[7] that Scrooge believed it was the same, until he saw *her*, now a comely matron, sitting opposite her daughter. The noise in this room was perfectly tumultuous, for there were more children there, than Scrooge in his agitated state of mind could count; and, unlike the celebrated herd in the poem, they were not forty children conducting themselves like one, but every child was conducting itself like forty.

The consequences were uproarious beyond belief; but no one seemed to care; on the contrary, the mother and daughter laughed heartily, and enjoyed it very much; and the latter, soon beginning to mingle in the sports, got pillaged by the young brigands most ruthlessly. What would I[8] not have given to be one of them! Though I never could have been so rude, no, no! I wouldn't for the wealth of all the world have crushed that braided hair, and torn it down; and for the precious little shoe, I wouldn't have plucked it off, God bless my soul! to save my life. As to measuring her waist in sport, as they did, bold young brood, I couldn't have done it; I should have expected my arm to have grown round it for a punishment, and never come straight again.

And yet I should have dearly liked, I own, to have touched her lips; to have questioned her, that she might have opened them; to have looked upon the lashes of her downcast eyes, and never raised a blush; to have let loose waves of hair, an inch of which would be a keepsake beyond price: in short, I should have liked, I do confess, to have had the lightest license of a child, and yet to have been man enough to know its value.

But now a knocking at the door was heard, and such a rush immediately ensued that she with laughing face and plundered dress was borne towards it the centre of a flushed and boisterous group, just in time to greet the father, who came home attended by a man laden with Christmas toys and presents. Then the shouting and the struggling, and the onslaught that was made on the defenceless porter! The scaling him with chairs for ladders to dive into his pockets, despoil him of brown-paper parcels, hold on tight by his cravat[9], hug him round his neck, pommel his back, and kick his legs in irrepressible affection! The shouts of wonder and delight with which the development of every package was received! The terrible announcement that the baby had been taken in the act of putting a doll's frying-pan into his mouth, and was more than

---

6 That is, Ebenezer Scrooge and the Ghost of Christmas Past.
7 That is, Scrooge's former sweetheart, now married to someone else and with children of her own.
8 That is, the narrator.

---

9 A kind of light scarf usually worn in place of a necktie for ornamentation rather than warmth.

suspected of having swallowed a fictitious turkey, glued on a wooden platter! The immense relief of finding this a false alarm! The joy, and gratitude, and ecstasy! They are all indescribable alike. It is enough that by degrees the children and their emotions got out of the parlour, and by one stair at a time, up to the top of the house; where they went to bed, and so subsided.

Questions #11-20 are based on Passages 1 and 2.

11. The author of Passage 1 emphasizes
    (A) how differences in social class affect the ways children treat one another.
    (B) the comical antics of boisterous children at Christmas.
    (C) the variety of playthings and gifts the children received.
    (D) his own hopes of making a business contact with the wealthy contractor.

12. The boisterousness of the children in Passage 2 results from a mood best described as
    (A) panicked and terrified.
    (B) agitated and anxious.
    (C) exuberant and joyful.
    (D) belligerent and aggressive.

13. Which choice provides the best evidence for the answer to the preceding question?
    (A) Line 96-99 ("The noise in … mind could count")
    (B) Line 106-109 ("but no one … it very much")
    (C) Line 133-137 ("in short, I … know its value")
    (D) Line 166-171 ("It is enough … and so subsided.")

14. As used in line 36, *discrimination* most nearly means
    (A) removal of accusations or criminal charges previously held against someone.
    (B) practice of denying goods or services to people of another race, sex, or class.
    (C) effectiveness of something that was done with the intend to educate.
    (D) skill in judging differences, especially in degree or quality.

15. The authors of both passages would most likely agree with which of the following statements?
    (A) Even at Christmas, adults should take a strong hand at reining in the excesses of their children's behavior.
    (B) Especially at Christmas, adults should let themselves cut loose and act like children.
    (C) In the excitement of Christmas, adults should not force children to sit still and be quiet.
    (D) Since Christmas is a religious holiday, Christmas celebrations should be staid and respectful.

16. As used in line 135, *license* most nearly means
    (A) the state of being infested with insects, especially in the hair.
    (B) a document granting a legal privilege, as to drive a vehicle or practice a trade.
    (C) freedom to act in a way that would otherwise be socially unacceptable.
    (D) abandonment of conscience and abdication of moral responsibility.

17. In Passage 1, what is the most likely reason that the red-haired boy "did not dare to cry" (lines 76-77)?
    (A) The other child did not hit him hard enough to hurt him.
    (B) He wanted to impress the pale, quiet girl by showing her how tough he was.
    (C) Because of his naturally stoic temperament, he did not often show his feelings.
    (D) Being poorer than the other children, he knew he did not really have the right to play with them.

18. Which choice provides the best evidence for the answer to the preceding question?
    (A) Lines 56-59 ("he longed to … understood his position")
    (B) Lines 60-62 ("I love watching … are extremely interesting.")
    (C) Lines 69-72 ("he gave away … pocket-handkerchief already")
    (D) Lines 83-85 ("She let him … the expensive doll.")

19. In the contexts of these two passages, the phrases "The children were all incredibly sweet" (Passage 1, line 1) and "pommel his back, and kick his legs" (Passage 2, line 153) exemplify which literary technique?
    (A) Simile
    (B) Irony
    (C) Personification
    (D) Alliteration

20. What is the most likely explanation for the differences in how the children interact with one another in these two passages?
    (A) The children in Passage 1 belong to families of different social classes, but the children in Passage 2 all belong to the same family.
    (B) Passage 1 takes place in a large house with many rooms, but Passage 2 takes place in one room in a modest house.
    (C) The gifts given to the children in Passage 1 were different from the gifts given to the children in Passage 2.
    (D) Passage 1 takes place in Russia while Passage 2 takes place in England, and children are raised differently in those two countries.

Practice Passage Three: A Passage with a Visual Aid

From his early years as a Philadelphia typesetter and printer's apprentice to his later career as U.S. Postmaster General and Ambassador to France, Benjamin Franklin is one of the best known and most beloved of the U.S. Founding Fathers. In this excerpt from his Autobiography, *the largely self-taught Franklin details his plan for moral self-improvement and explains how he devised a chart to track his progress.*

In the various enumerations of the moral virtues I had met with in my reading, I found the catalogue more or less numerous, as different writers included more or fewer ideas under the same name. Temperance, for example, was by some confined to eating and drinking, while by others it was extended to mean the moderating every other pleasure, appetite, inclination, or passion, bodily or mental, even to our avarice and ambition. I propos'd to myself, for the sake of clearness, to use rather more names, with fewer ideas annex'd to each, than a few names with more ideas; and I included under thirteen names of virtues all that at that time occurr'd to me as necessary or desirable, and annexed to each a short precept, which fully express'd the extent I gave to its meaning. …

My intention being to acquire the *habitude* of all these virtues, I judg'd it would be well not to distract my attention by attempting the whole at once, but to fix it on one of them at a time; and, when I should be master of that, then to proceed to another, and so on, till I should have gone thro' the thirteen; and, as the previous acquisition of some might facilitate the acquisition of certain others, I arrang'd them with that view, as they stand above. Temperance first, as it tends to procure that coolness and clearness of head, which is so necessary where constant vigilance was to be kept up, and guard maintained against the unremitting attraction of ancient habits, and the force of perpetual temptations. This being acquir'd and establish'd, Silence would be more easy; and my desire being to gain knowledge at the same time that I improv'd in virtue, and considering that in conversation it was obtain'd rather by the use of the ears than of the tongue, and therefore wishing to break a habit I was getting into of prattling, punning, and joking, which only made me acceptable to trifling company, I gave *Silence* the second place. This and the next, *Order*, I expected would allow me more time for attending to my project and my studies. *Resolution*, once become habitual, would keep me firm in my endeavours to obtain all the subsequent virtues; *Frugality* and Industry freeing me from my remaining debt, and producing affluence and independence, would make more easy the practice of Sincerity and Justice, etc., etc. Conceiving then, that, agreeably to the advice of Pythagoras in his Golden Verses, daily examination would be necessary, I contriv'd the following method for conducting that examination.

I made a little book, in which I allotted a page for each of the virtues. I rul'd each page with red ink, so as to have seven columns, one for each day of the week, marking each column with a letter for the day. I cross'd these columns with thirteen red lines, marking the beginning of each line with the first letter of one of the virtues, on which line, and in its proper column, I might mark, by a little black spot, every fault I found upon examination to have been committed respecting that virtue upon that day.

I determined to give a week's strict attention to each of the virtues successively. Thus, in the first week, my great guard was to avoid every the least offense against Temperance, leaving the other virtues to their ordinary chance, only marking every evening the faults of the day. Thus, if in the first week I could keep my first line, marked T, clear of spots, I suppos'd the habit of that virtue so much strengthen'd, and its opposite weaken'd, that I might venture extending my attention to include the next, and for the following week keep both lines clear of spots. Proceeding thus to the last, I could go thro' a course compleat in thirteen weeks, and four courses in a year. And like him who, having a garden to weed, does not attempt to eradicate all the bad herbs at once, which would exceed his reach and his strength, but works on one of the beds at a time, and, having accomplish'd the first, proceeds to a second, so I should have, I hoped, the encouraging pleasure of seeing on my pages the progress I made in virtue, by clearing successively my lines of their spots, till in the end, by a number of courses, I should be happy in viewing a clean book, after a thirteen weeks' daily examination.

Form of the pages.

TEMPERANCE.							
EAT NOT TO DULLNESS DRINK NOT TO ELEVATION.							
	S.	M.	T.	W.	T.	F.	S.
T.							
S.	*	*		*		*	
O.	**	*	*		*	*	*
R.			*			*	
F.		*			*		
I.			*				
S.							
J.							
M.							
C.							
T.							
C.							
H.							
J.							

In this chart, the columns represent days of the week. The first thirteen rows, in order from top to bottom, represent the virtues of Temperance, Silence, Order, Resolution, Frugality, Industry, Sincerity, Justice, Moderation, Cleanliness, Tranquility, Chastity, and Humility; what the "J" in the fourteenth row signifies is not clear from the text of the Autobiography.

Questions #21-30 are based on the previous passage.

21. Franklin most likely wrote this passage in order to
    (A) critique other authors' descriptions of moral virtues.
    (B) explain how his early cultivation of moral virtues led to his later success.
    (C) outline a plan by which anyone can become more virtuous.
    (D) illustrate his own ingenuity in devising a plan for moral self-improvement.

22. Which choice provides the best evidence for the answer to the previous question?
    (A) Lines 1-6 ("In the various ... the same name.")
    (B) Lines 31-35 ("as the previous ... they stand above")
    (C) Lines 69-70 ("I contrived the ... conducting that examination.")
    (D) Lines 85-87 ("I determined to ... the virtues successively.")

23. Which of the following best explains why Franklin listed the virtues in the order he did?
    (A) One of the books he read listed them in that order.
    (B) He thought that having certain virtues would make the practice of certain others easier.
    (C) He believed in cultivating the most important virtue first.
    (D) He believed in building up to the most important virtue and cultivating it last.

24. As used in line 36, *coolness* most nearly means
    (A) freedom from excitability.
    (B) social desirability.
    (C) low body temperature.
    (D) a slang term for "money."

25. Franklin's reference to going through four courses of his self-improvement program in a year (lines 101-103) most strongly suggests which of the following?
    (A) He thought he would enjoy his program and want to repeat it.
    (B) He did not expect his program to eradicate all his vices the first time through.
    (C) He did not expect his program to do him much good, but he lacked any better ideas.
    (D) He wanted a yearlong program but could not think of thirty-nine more virtues to work on.

26. The graphic was most likely included to
    (A) demonstrate how Franklin had an easier time with virtues on some days than on others.
    (B) show that Order was the most difficult virtue for Franklin to master.
    (C) illustrate Franklin's method for keeping track of his moral failings.
    (D) provide readers with a template to use in their own self-improvement efforts.

27. Franklin would most likely agree with which of the following?
    (A) The acquisition of virtues does not happen overnight.
    (B) Ancient Greek writers like Pythagoras are the best sources of knowledge about virtues.
    (C) There are thirteen and only thirteen virtues which are important.
    (D) Strict record-keeping is the best approach to solving a problem.

28. Which choice provides the best evidence for the answer to the previous question?
    (A) Lines 13-16 ("I propos'd to … with more ideas")
    (B) Lines 23-28 ("My intention being … at a time")
    (C) Lines 80-84 ("on which line … upon that day")
    (D) Lines 103-113 ("And like him … made in virtue")

29. As used in line 61, *Industry* most nearly means
    (A) an early form of manufacturing work.
    (B) a disposition toward working hard.
    (C) Franklin's financial stake in a business endeavor.
    (D) acquisitiveness, especially with regard to money.

30. It can be reasonably inferred from the passage that
    (A) by following this plan, Franklin succeeded in making himself virtuous.
    (B) the order in which Franklin listed the virtues is the most sensible order for everyone.
    (C) moral self-improvement plans such as Franklin's were common in the 1700s.
    (D) Franklin wanted his readers to think of him as resourceful, industrious, and a lover of virtue.

Reading Practice Set Answers

1. B
2. D
3. C
4. A
5. D
6. D
7. A
8. B
9. C
10. B
11. A
12. C
13. B
14. D
15. C
16. C
17. D
18. A
19. B
20. A
21. D
22. C
23. B
24. A
25. B
26. C
27. A
28. D
29. B
30. D

Chapter 4: The Writing and Language Test

Overview

The Writing and Language Test on the new SAT is straightforward in its format, but complex in its content. That means that most students preparing for this test will just need to focus on reviewing rules of English grammar and style, as well as brushing up on composition and editing skills.

This chapter contains explanations of the Writing and Language Test and its questions. The two chapters that follow it include a parts of speech glossary to help you brush up on your grammar, over a dozen topic-specific modules to help you with everything from dangling participles to subject-verb agreement, and practice passages accompanied by realistic test questions. You will emerge from those pages like a linguistic butterfly with a new sense of enlightenment about the English language! Hopefully. Probably.

For now, about the Writing Test…

How will the test be set up?

You will be given 35 minutes to complete the Writing and Language Test. It will contain four passages of about 400-450 words each, written specifically for the SAT. Each passage will be accompanied by eleven multiple-choice questions (for a total of 44 questions on the test). Each question will have four answer choices.

Four passages and 44 questions in 35 minutes? That seems like an intimidating task! But here's what you need to know:

- The passages will include one each of the following topics: Careers, Humanities, Science, and Social Studies/History. The passages may include persuasive, informative, or narrative tones.

- Most of the questions will refer to an underlined word, phrase, or sentence in the text and ask you to determine whether it is effective as-is or to select the best correction from three alternatives.

- Some questions will ask you about larger sections of the text, the logic or composition of the passage, or the passage as a whole.

- A little over half (24 of 44) of the questions will focus upon the Expression of Ideas in the passages—issues of argument development, organization, and use of language. The rest of the questions (20 of 44) will focus upon Standard English Conventions: sentence structure, grammar usage, and punctuation.

Question Types

Most of the questions in the Writing and Language Test will follow the same format. Each question will identify a specific underlined part of the passage and present you with four ways that underlined part can be written: the version in the passage (written as "NO CHANGE") and three alternative versions. You will then be asked to choose the best of those four options.

A few questions may vary that format a bit, such as by presenting a new piece of information and asking how a part of the passage should be written in light of that new information, but the basic idea is the same. You'll still be choosing the best of four ways to write a part of the passage.

The questions in the Writing and Language Test will come in two broad categories: 20 of them will focus on Standard English Conventions, and 24 of them will focus on the Expression of Ideas. (The question types won't be labeled on the test, but you'll probably be able to figure out which questions are which type based on what they're asking.)

Standard English Conventions Questions

These questions deal with exactly the sort of issues you'd expect them to deal with: punctuation, usage, and sentence structure. They will include, among other topics:

- proper use of colons, semicolons, apostrophes, commas, and other marks
- agreement between pronouns and antecedents or between subjects and verbs
- frequently confused words and idiomatic expressions
- sentence fragments and run-on sentences
- parallelism and comparisons
- modifiers
- verb tenses
- clause coordination and subordination
- mood, voice, and tone

You can read in greater detail about specific conventions of written English—and practice your skills—in Chapter 5, starting on page 47.

Expression of Ideas Questions

If the Standard English Conventions questions deal with how *correct* the writing in the passage is, then the Expression of Ideas questions deal with how *effective* the writing in the passage is. To answer the Expression of Ideas questions, you'll have to be able to assess the organization of the passage, the development of ideas, and the effective use of language. That means the issues you'll have to consider will include topics like:

- whether the passage presents ideas and information in the most logical order
- how effectively the passage transitions from one idea to the next
- whether elements like main ideas and topic sentences give the text an appropriate structure

- how effectively the ideas and information in the passage support the main argument

- how relevant the ideas and information in the passage are to its overall purpose

- how quantitative information in graphs and tables relates to the text

- how precise and suitable the words in the passage are

- whether the passage is concise or wordy

- how well the sentence structure serves the overall purpose of the passage

- whether the tone and style are consistent and suited to the passage's purpose

As you can see, these questions will rely less on your knowledge of the rules of writing and more on your logical and analytical skills. Those skills are best developed through regular reading—and active reading. For more on what active reading means and how to do it effectively, refer to Chapter 2.

How to Get Through the Questions

Here are three key strategies to keep in mind as you prepare for the Writing and Language Test. You can practice these strategies with the Writing and Language Practice Set in Chapter 6, beginning on page 101.

First, for each passage and problem set, quickly read through *the whole passage* with your pencil in hand. You can circle or mark any errors that jump out at you on that first read-through, but the main goal is to get a sense of the passage's main topic and key details.

- You do *not* need to read this passage as "actively" as you would a passage on the Reading or Essay tests—no need for note-taking—but you can still mark the main topic if you find it helpful to do so.

- Marking any potential errors you spot on that first read-through will help you to move through the questions faster. Think of the read-through as mental stretching before you sprint through the questions; you'll "run" better if you've prepared your mind for the race ahead!

Second, for each question remember that you are seeking not only an answer that is grammatically correct, but also the one that results in the *best and most effective* sentence and the *best and most effective* passage overall.

- When you read an underlined portion in a sentence, try to identify an error within it (e.g., wrong pronoun, mismatched subject and verb, etc.). If you spot one, you'll already be down to three answer choices, since "(A) NO CHANGE" will be incorrect.

- Eliminate any answer choices that don't correct the error you spotted, and choose the best (most concise and clear) answer that remains.

- If you don't spot an error, don't panic! Some questions will be correct as written. Just read through answers **B**, **C**, and **D** to see if any of them improves the original sentence. If not, then choose "(A) NO CHANGE" with confidence and move on.

Third, for any question (usually an Expression of Ideas question) that asks you for something hypothetical, like which additional detail would most improve the passage, *slow down and try them out*.

- It would take too much of your time to read every version of *every* answer choice on *every* question on the Writing and Language Test, but when the larger context of the passage is important, it's definitely worth it.

- If you are stuck between two or more answer choices, move on from that question. Answer everything else for the passage and then return to that question. Working through the rest of the passage's questions might help to clarify omitted questions. Just like on the Reading Test, you will avoid confusion if you try to answer any remaining questions for a passage before getting into the next passage.

A Final Note

Overall, for the Writing and Language Test, you should aim to be **efficient** with your time, **attentive** to the questions, and **confident** in your answer choices. Following the strategies above will help you to do just that!

Chapter 5: Grammar and Style Review

Overview

Think of this chapter as a virtual training ground for the basic grammatical and stylistic concepts you'll need to grasp for the SAT Writing and Language Test. In addition to systematic explanations of the concepts, you will find drills to practice your newly honed skills. For your reference, here is a list of all the sections and modules contained in this chapter:

- Grammar and Parts of Speech Glossary
- Coordination and Subordination
- Run-Ons and Fragments
- Parallelism and Comparisons
- Modifiers (Adjectives and Adverbs)
- Participles
- Pronouns
- Noun and Subject-Verb Agreement
- Verb Tenses
- Word Choice and Idioms
- Common Punctuation Issues

Work through them in order if you want a thorough review of all the essentials… or if you're pressed for time, start with the topics you know you need to review the most. We hope that you find this chapter instructive and helpful!

Grammar and Parts of Speech Glossary

You will not need to identify parts of speech or grammatical terms on the Writing and Language Test, but this glossary is included as a reference. We encourage you to use it to help you understand structures of sentences, as well as the terms used throughout the grammar and style drills that follow.

Adjective: a word that describes a noun; a "what" modifier.
*My **older** sister has a **bad** habit of playing **loud** music.*

Adverb: a word that describes a verb, an adjective, or another adverb; a "how" modifier.
*The **slightly** clumsy horse trotted **unevenly** into the **very** old barn.*

Article: a word that introduces a noun; also known as a determiner. "The" is the definite article, and "a/an" is the indefinite article.
*A dog is **the** best friend **a** child can have.*

Clause: a combination of words that includes a subject and a predicate verb to express a thought. An independent clause expresses a complete thought. A dependent/subordinate clause expresses a thought that depends upon another clause to complete it.
  __Independent__: I went to the store.
  __Dependent__: Because I went to the store,

Comma Splice: the improper use of a comma to join two independent clauses; also known as a type of run-on sentence.
*I like to play Monopoly with my **family, we** stop once one of us goes bankrupt.*

Comparative: an adjective that compares the noun in question to others, always used when comparing two items.
*Of the two sisters, Elsa was **wiser**, but Anna was **braver**.*

Conjunction: a word that joins two or more words or phrases. FANBOYS conjunctions (for, and, nor, but, or, yet, and so) can be used to join independent clauses with a comma.
*Sarah **and** Ava wish they could come to the movie with us, **but** they're both grounded.*

Determiner: a word that introduces a noun; also known as an article (see above).

Exclamation: a word or phrase that demonstrates strong emotion, typically followed by an exclamation mark; also known as an interjection.
*"**Whoa!**" said Eric. "That car almost rear-ended us. **Yikes!**"*

Fragment: a clause or phrase that does not express a complete thought. A dependent (or subordinate) clause is a kind of fragment.
   Despite the proliferation of frozen yogurt restaurants in our city.

Gerund: the "ing" form of a verb.
   Examples: *running, wearing, juggling, talking, thinking, etc.*

Idiom: a standard word, phrase, or expression that must be used in a fixed and certain way to be correct; these are not based upon grammar rules, but upon cultural context and evolved standards. The SAT does not test colloquial idioms such as "at the drop of a hat" and "she broke up with me"; it does test prepositional and gerund/infinitive idioms.
   Correct: *After a long debate, the committee **agreed upon** a course of action.*
   Incorrect: *After a long debate, the committee **agreed with** a course of action.*

In the example above, the wrong preposition changes the meaning of the sentence; you agree *upon* a decision that you make, but agree *with* a decision made by someone else. These types of idioms hinge upon the use of the correct preposition or verb form, and they often "just sound wrong" if they are incorrect.
   Correct: *In my free time I enjoy crocheting.*
   Incorrect: *In my free time I enjoy **to crochet**.*

For a detailed discussion of idioms, review the module beginning on page 83.

Infinitive: the "to" form of a verb.
   Examples: *to swim, to sleep, to dance, etc.*

Interjection: a word or phrase that interrupts, often with strong emotion; also known as an exclamation (see above).

Modifier: a word that changes or describes another word. Adjectives, adverbs, participles, and phrases are all types of modifiers.
   ***Trying to finish his drawing**, Jackie reached **quickly** for the **blue** crayon.*

Noun: a person, place, thing, or idea. Proper nouns are capitalized and used for names, places, groups, and honorifics.
   ***Claude Monet** is perhaps the best-known **pioneer** of French **Impressionism**.*

Object: the part of a sentence or phrase that is acted upon by the verb. Direct objects typically follow the verb, and indirect objects are usually joined to the verb by a preposition.
   Direct: *The glass slipper fit Cinderella's **foot** perfectly.*
   Indirect: *Prince Charming immediately proposed **to Cinderella**.*

Participle: a verb that functions as an adjective; it provides description rather than action. Present participles end in "ing" (the gerund form); past participles end in regular ("-ed," "-en," etc) or irregular forms ("bought," "swum," etc). Participial phrases begin with participles.

> <u>**Running** to the door</u>, he tripped over the toys <u>**left** in the hallway</u>. (Participial phrases underlined)

Phrase: a group of words that function together within a sentence but do not express a complete thought.

> **To be honest**, the suggestion **of wearing** a winter coat sounds like **a real pain**.

Predicate Verb: a verb that expresses the main action of a clause or sentence.

> Amy **went** to the networking event because she **intended** to change jobs soon.

Preposition: a word that describes a relationship to other words, usually in terms of literal or figurative proximity. Prepositional phrases begin with prepositions.

> If you're looking **for** the leftover Halloween candy, check **on** top **of** the refrigerator, **behind** the cookie tins.

Pronoun: a word that is used in place of a noun. Subjective pronouns (I, you, he, she, they, we, who) take the place of subjects, while objective pronouns (me, you, him, her, them, us, whom) take the place of objects. Possessive pronouns (my, your, his, her, their, our) show ownership.

> **He** and Josh said **they** were coming to **my** party with Molly and **her**.

Less commonly tested pronouns include the following types. They may look like adjectives, but these words are pronouns if they are being used in place of nouns.

> *Demonstrative*: used to distinguish a noun (that, this, these, those).
>
> *Indefinite*: used to refer to something general or nonspecific (all, any, both, each, everyone, few, many, neither, none, nothing, several, some, somebody).
>
> *Intensive*: used to emphasize its antecedent (herself, himself, itself, myself, ourselves, themselves, yourselves).
>
> *Interrogative*: used to ask a question (what, whatever, who, whoever, where, wherever, when, whenever).
>
> *Reflexive*: used to refer to the subject of a sentence (herself, himself, itself, myself, ourselves, themselves, yourselves).
>
> *Relative*: used to introduce a new clause (that, which, who, whom).

Run-On: a sentence in which two independent clauses are improperly joined. Run-ons can usually be fixed with a comma and a conjunction, or with a properly used semicolon.
>   *Incorrect: The Steelers play well against most teams they struggle against the Seahawks.*
>   *Correct: The Steelers play well against most teams**,** **but** they struggle against the Seahawks.*

Sentence: a group of words that includes a subject and a predicate verb and expresses a complete thought.
>   *After a long day at the amusement park,* ***Emmeline wanted*** *to go home.*

Subject: the part of a sentence or phrase that carries out the action. The subject may not be the noun closest to the verb.
>   *The best **part** of superhero movies is the moment when the **hero** saves an ordinary citizen.*

Superlative: an adjective expressing the highest degree that compares the noun in question to others, always used when comparing three or more items.
>   *On any given rollercoaster, the back row is the **best** for thrill-seekers.*

Tense: the construction of a verb that describes when it occurs in time. The three simple tenses are past, present, and future. Also commonly tested are the perfect tenses. For a more detailed discussion of tenses, review the module beginning on page 79.
>   *Past: Christopher Columbus **sailed** to the Americas in 1492.*
>   *Present: We **learn** interesting facts about early exploration history in school.*
>   *Future: The question of who "discovered" North America **will continue** to be debated.*
>   *Past Perfect: Columbus **had run** out of funding before the Spanish monarchs backed him.*
>   *Present Perfect: The exploration of the Americas **has remained** fascinating to historians.*
>   *Future Perfect: By the time I run out of Christopher Columbus-related sentences, we **will have reviewed** all the basic tenses.*

Verb: a word that describes an action, state, or event.
>   *Before you **leave**, please **sort** the laundry, **close** the windows, and **set** the alarm.*

Coordination and Subordination

Think of clauses within sentences as two people running an old-fashioned "three-legged race." The clauses need something to hold them together and make sure they're going in the same direction. This is what coordination and subordination do.

When you have multiple clauses working together in a sentence, you must join them so that the sentence completes a logical thought. Which of these sentences makes more sense to you?

Since Amelia couldn't join us for the concert, we decided to go anyway.

Although Amelia couldn't join us for the concert, we decided to go anyway.

In both cases the first clause is *dependent* or *subordinate*, meaning that it doesn't complete a thought or action on its own but instead depends upon the action in the second clause. However, the first sentence doesn't make sense; it's saying that we decided to go anyway *because* Amelia couldn't join us, when logically we decided to go *even though* she couldn't. The second sentence correctly expresses that contrast.

Rule 1: Coordinating conjunctions, or FANBOYS conjunctions (**F**or, **A**nd, **N**or, **B**ut, **O**r, **Y**et, **S**o), are used to join independent clauses. They can also be used to fix run-on sentences. When used to join two clauses, coordinating conjunctions require a comma *before* the conjunction.

    Examples: David wanted pizza for dinner, ***but*** Grant voted for barbecue.

                       Well, I asked her to prom, ***and*** she said she'd think about it.

                       Koalas are often called "koala bears," ***yet*** they are not bears.

Rule 2: Subordinating conjunctions can also be used to join independent clauses and correct run-on sentences. Common subordinating conjunctions include: after, although, as, because, before, even if, if, since, that, though, unless, until, when, where, wherever, whether, and while. If the subordinate clause begins a sentence, a comma must follow it.

    Examples: Iron Man is the best superhero ***because*** he is resourceful and smart.

                       Even if you text him, Jon will not respond ***when*** he is fishing.

                       After shots were fired at Fort Sumter, the Civil War began.

Practice: Choose the correct conjunction for each sentence. Mark your choice with a "C" if it is a coordinating conjunction or "S" if it is a subordinating conjunction.

S 1. (**After** / If) I studied Spanish to the point of fluency, I decided to start learning Mandarin.

C 2. Caroline passed me the water bottle, (**and** / for) I took a long drink.

S 3. It can be difficult to study for tests like the SAT (where / **when**) you have so many other commitments and responsibilities.

S 4. My mother always told me to think (because / **before**) I speak.

C 5. We have given the guilty party multiple chances to come forward, (**yet** / or) no one has.

S 6. (**Since** / While) my little brother needed to use the bathroom, we stopped at a gas station.

C 7. The doorbell rang, (**and** / but) the dog barked loudly.

S 8. (Before / **While**) Liam was busy learning to juggle, Erika decided to attempt the trapeze.

S 9. (**Although** / Because) Romeo and Juliet's families bitterly hated each other, the young couple fell in love.

C 10. You told me that you like horses, (but / **so**) I assumed that you also like unicorns.

Answers

1. After – S
2. And – C
3. When – S
4. Before – S
5. Yet – C
6. Since – S
7. And – C
8. While – S
9. Although – S
10. So – C

Run-Ons and Fragments

Run-on sentences and fragments cause similar types of problems in sentences. In order for a sentence to be complete, it must have a subject and a predicate (acting) verb *and* express a complete thought. For example: "Lauren likes to drink hot apple cider."

A fragment may have a subject and predicate verb, but it does not express a complete thought. For example: "Although Lauren likes to drink hot apple cider."

A run-on sentence expresses two or more thoughts that are improperly joined. For example: "Lauren likes to drink apple cider, she prefers hot cider."

Rule 1: Identify a fragment by finding a subject-verb combination and checking whether it expresses a complete thought. If it *is* a fragment, correct it by removing any words that make it an unfinished thought (such as a subordinating conjunction) or by adding words to form a complete, logical sentence. Correcting fragments is all about **completing**.

> Examples: *Incorrect*: Eric running to the bus stop. *(No predicate verb)*
>
> *Correct*: Eric **was** running to the bus stop.
>
> *Incorrect*: Because you got a haircut. *(Incomplete thought)*
>
> *Correct*: Because you got a haircut, **I got one too**.

Rule 2: Identify a run-on by checking for subject-verb combinations and determining whether the clauses are properly joined. If the clauses are joined by a comma with no conjunction (this error is called a "comma splice"), or with nothing at all, then it's a run-on. Correct it by joining the clauses with a comma *and* a conjunction, a semicolon, or a period (to split them into separate sentences). Correcting run-ons is all about **combining**.

> Examples: *Incorrect*: The rabbit jumped right in front of our car, I swerved to avoid hitting it. *(Comma without a conjunction = comma splice)*
>
> *Correct*: The rabbit jumped in front of our car, **but** I swerved to avoid hitting it. *(Comma + conjunction = two properly combined clauses)*
>
> *Also Correct*: **When** the rabbit jumped in front of our car, I swerved to avoid hitting it. *(Conjunction + comma = properly combined)*

Practice: Read the sentences that follow. Mark each fragment with "F" and each run-on with "R," then rewrite to correct the error. If a sentence is correct as it is, then mark it with "C."

F 1. Despite the fact that I disagree with almost everything you just said, ~~I~~ I agree with your last point.

F 2. Alissa ~~checking~~ checked Facebook ~~while~~ while she rode the train to work each morning.

C 3. I was never a fan of baseball until I went to a game and watched it in person.

R 4. Braxton caught the football quickly and easily. then He took off for the end zone.

F 5. The hardest things about babysitting toddlers are feeding them and changing diapers.

C 6. The skyscraper was actually built to sway in the wind; its height made this feature necessary.

R 7. Holly and Libby realized they had bought the same dress for the homecoming dance, but neither of them was willing to exchange it for something else.

R 8. You should ask Theo to tell you his story about the time that a live bear got into the mall. It's unbelievable!

R 9. I ignored the ringing phone, because I was getting sick of telemarketers.

F 10. The day Zayn left One Direction is known as Black Wednesday in my house.

Answers:

1. Fragment – remove "despite the fact that" to complete the sentence.
2. Fragment – replace "checking" with "***checked***" to complete the sentence.
3. Correct as written.
4. Run-on – suggested change: "Braxton caught the football quickly and easily ***and*** took off for the end zone."
5. Fragment – suggested change: "The hardest things about babysitting toddlers ***are*** feeding them and changing diapers."
6. Correct as written.
7. Run-on – add the word "but" or "yet" after the comma to combine the clauses.
8. Run-on – replace the comma with a semicolon or period.
9. Run-on – replace the comma with a semicolon or subordinating conjunction like "because" to combine the clauses.
10. Fragment – change "known" to "***is*** known" to complete the sentence.

Parallelism and Comparisons

In the English language, certain standards exist for the structure of sentences. These standards include the organization of comparisons and series into like terms, and the SAT often tests these standards by mixing them up. Which of these sentences makes more immediate sense to you?

> *At summer camp I learned how to tie knots, tend a campfire, and they also taught me to pitch a tent.*
>
> *At summer camp I learned how to tie knots, tend a campfire, and pitch a tent.*

The second sentence is correct because it applies parallel structure to the three verb forms—"tie," "tend," and "pitch"—without the unnecessary mess of a new subject and action ("they also taught"). It is easier for the reader to organize the actions of the sentence. Here are three commonly tested rules regarding comparisons and parallelism:

Rule 1: When comparing two people or things, use the *comparative* form of an adjective (-er or "more"). When comparing three or more people or things, use the *superlative* form of an adjective (-est or "most").

> Examples: Kayla is **more knowledgeable** about botany than Chloe is.
>
> Among my three brothers, Zach is the **oldest**.
>
> Professor Snape was the **harshest** and **most difficult** of all Harry's teachers.

Rule 2: When comparing or listing things, make sure that the items match in number, verb tense, and structure. People must be compared to people, places to places, actions to actions, and so on.

> Examples: I prefer the **music** of Wiz Khalifa to **that** of Flo Rida.
>
> Before you leave, make sure that you have **turned off** the lights, **adjusted** the air conditioning, and **locked** the door.
>
> Of the twins, Hailey was **the faster**, but Zoe was **the stronger**.

Rule 3: Sometimes parallel structures will depend upon "joining" idiom pairs such as either/or, neither/nor, not only/but also, both/and, between/and, etc. Think of these idioms like bookends—you need both of the pieces to keep the sentence structure in place.

> Examples: The film was ***not only*** less engaging than expected, ***but also*** less amusing.
>
> ***Neither*** Lucy ***nor*** Peter knows where Edmund has gone.
>
> Tim dreams ***both of going*** bungee jumping ***and of swimming*** with sharks.

*Note on that last one that the actions fall within the **both/and** structure ("both of going... and of swimming").*

*Anything that's outside the "joining" structure applies to everything that's inside it, so "Tim dreams **of both going** bungee jumping **and swimming** with sharks" would also be correct. We don't need a second "of," because the first one applies to both of Tim's dreams.*

Practice: Correct any errors in the following sentences. If the sentence is correct as written, mark it with a "C."

1. Of the Jones triplets, Cayden is the ~~younger~~ [youngest] by two minutes.

2. That was the worst car trip I have ever taken.

3. While you're in the museum, consider the difference between Van Gogh's brushstrokes and [those of] Monet.

C 4. The undeniable benefits of regular exercise include improved circulation, lowered body-mass index, and increased lifespan.

5. Neither Grayson ~~or~~ [nor] his brother Sawyer knew where their mother had left her keys.

C 6. Ms. Lopez considered the music video to be both bizarre and unsettling.

7. The bag of Halloween candy was unevenly divided between Katelyn and Jenna; Katelyn received ~~the most~~ [more] by at least a dozen pieces.

8. The story of Mariah Carey's discovery by a record executive is more remarkable than [that of] almost any other recording artist.

9. I invited you to come to the farm with me not only to pick apples, but also ~~for the walking~~ [to walk] through of the corn maze.

10. Before we can turn on the football game, I have to mow the lawn, put away the folded laundry, and [empty] the clean dishes from the dishwasher.

Answers:

1. Replace "younger" with "youngest."
2. Replace "worse" with "worst."
3. Replace "Monet" with "Monet's brushstrokes" or "those of Monet."
4. Correct as written.
5. Replace "or" with "nor."
6. Correct as written.
7. Replace "the most" with "more."
8. Insert "the story of" or "that of" before "almost any other recording artist."
9. Replace "for the walking through of" with "to walk through."
10. Replace "the clean dishes from" with "unload" or similar verb.

Modifiers (Adjectives and Adverbs)

Without modifiers, the English-speaking world would be a pretty vague place. Modifiers—specifically adjectives and adverbs—provide illustrative, clarifying, and emphatic details to sentences. They make our language (literally) more colorful and precise! For instance, consider these two sentences:

My sister's soccer team won the championship last year.

*My **youngest** sister's **gifted** soccer team **easily** won the **coveted** championship last year.*

See how the second sentence (with modifiers in bold) adds details to make the sentence more interesting and complex? Granted, reading an entire essay written like that would get a little exhausting—modifiers are best used in moderation. The key SAT skills to take away from this section are how to use modifiers properly and how to recognize when they are used improperly.

Rule 1: Adjectives are "what" modifiers, providing additional details of appearance, quality, or kind. Adjectives are used only to modify nouns or words functioning as nouns.

  Examples: I was awakened from a ***pleasant*** dream by the ***loud*** arguing of my ***grouchy*** neighbors.

        Paul prefers ***sweet*** gummy bears to ***tart*** Sour Patch Kids.

        The bronco dodged the ***quick*** swinging of the lariat.

*Note that even though "swing" is a verb, the adjective "quick" describes "swinging" because it's an **action** that is being described; it functions like a noun.*

Rule 2: Adverbs are "how" modifiers, describing degrees of intensity, relativity, or time. Adverbs can modify verbs, adjectives, and other adverbs, and they often end in -ly.

  Examples: Will ran ***very quickly*** towards the ***recently*** cleaned pool.

        (How did Will run? Quickly. How quickly? Very quickly. When was the pool cleaned? Recently.)

        You must drive ***cautiously*** at all times.

        (How must you drive? Cautiously.)

Practice: In the following sentences, draw an arrow from each modifier to the word it modifies.

1. What is the fastest way to get around that big canyon?

2. Nearing retirement, the already grumpy manager became positively nasty.

3. "That's really too kind of you," the duchess said lightly.

4. The heart of a hummingbird, though tiny, is surprisingly robust.

5. The expectant mother had an insatiable craving for French fries.

6. Taran honestly has become like a big brother to me.

Correct any errors in the following sentences. If the sentence is correct as written, mark it with a "C."

7. The fortune-teller, heavily veiled, insisted that I was destined to be a puppeteer.

C 8. You must be very cautious when approaching an elephant.

9. Regina's favorite drink at the coffee shop is a ~~frostily~~ frosty caramel-coffee milkshake.

10. No matter how cautiously you approach an elephant, it could still startle and charge you.

C 11. When my sinuses cleared, I could smell well again and noticed that the lilacs smelled good.

12. The doctor based her prescription of mild painkillers on the patient's statement that he was feeling ~~good~~ well.

13. Dominic always orders his latte extra hot so that it is still warm when he gets to work.

Answers:

1. "Fastest" (adjective) → "way"; "big" (adj) → "canyon" (noun)

2. "Already" (adverb) → "grumpy" (adj) → "manager" (n); "positively" (adv) → "nasty" (adj) → "manager" (n)

3. "Really" (adv) → "too" (adv) → "kind" (adj) → "that" (n); "lightly" (adv) → "said" (verb)

4. "Tiny" (adj) → "heart" (n); "surprisingly" (adv) → "robust" (adj) → "heart" (n)

5. "Expectant" (adj) → "mother" (n); "insatiable" (adj) → "craving" (n)

6. "Honestly" (adv) → "has" (v); "big" (adj) → "brother" (n)

7. Change "heavy" to "heavily" because it modifies *how* the fortune-teller was veiled.

8. Correct as written; "cautious" describes *what* you must be.

9. Change "frostily" to "frosty" because it modifies the noun "milkshake," not the adjectives that precede it.

10. Change "cautious" to "cautiously" because it modifies *how* you approach the elephant.

11. Correct as written; "well" is an adverb that describes *how* your nose smells, but "good" is an adjective that describes *what* the lilacs smell like to you.

12. Change "good" to "well" because it modifies *how* the patient was feeling.

13. Change "hotly" to "hot" because it modifies the noun "latte," not how Dominic places his order.

Participles

The previous section discussed adjectives and adverbs, both common modifiers. Participles are modifiers, too—they are **verbs that function as adjectives** within a sentence. Does that concept sound strange and confusing? Well, hang in there! It's going to make a lot more sense by the bottom of this page. Start by checking out this sentence:

> The **singing** bird perched on the **swaying** branch of the tree **turning** red under the autumn sky.

"Singing," "swaying," and "turning" are all verbs, but none of them is the predicate verb (main action) of the sentence. What's the main action? "The bird perched on the branch." The other three verbs are **participles**—they describe the nouns "bird," "branch," and "tree," respectively.

Rule 1: Present participles always end in –ing (also known as the **gerund** form of a verb), while past participles can end in a variety of regular (-ed, -en, -t) and irregular forms (rung, swum, etc.)

Examples: That stylishly **dressed** woman **waving** at us is my Aunt Rachel.

   Diving for the football, the player made an incredible catch.

   Riley prefers vegetables **grown** organically to those **sold** in most stores.

Rule 2: Participles can be used on their own or to begin **participial phrases**, which include additional information. In the sentence at the beginning of this section, "<u>**turning red**</u>" is a participial phrase.

Examples: <u>**Baked** to perfection</u>, the apple pie was the best that I had ever tasted.

   Sorry to catch you <u>**running** out the door</u>; do you have a minute?

   <u>**Retying** his shoelace</u>, Barrett found gum <u>**stuck** to his shoe</u>.

Rule 3: Participles are like magnets—they attach to, or describe, whatever noun is closest to them. When a participle begins a sentence, it describes the sentence's subject. A *dangling participle* occurs when a participle or participial phrase is placed so that it modifies the wrong thing.

Examples:

*<u>**Falling** from the sky</u>*, Jamie serenely admired the snowflakes. *(Incorrect: logically, the **snowflakes** are falling, not Jamie!)*

Jamie serenely admired the snowflakes *<u>**falling** from the sky</u>*. *(Correct: the participial phrase now immediately follows the noun it is intended to modify.)*

The advertisement was sponsored by the campaign, *<u>**considered** quite offensive</u>* to several minority organizations. *(Incorrect: this sentence says that the campaign is considered quite offensive, when logically it is the **advertisement**.)*

The advertisement *<u>**considered** quite offensive</u>* to several minority organizations was sponsored by the campaign. *(Correct: the participial phrase now connects directly to the advertisement.)*

Cecil's Tips to Stay Sharp

To check if a sentence has a dangling participle, try to picture it literally as it's written. An incorrect sentence will often provide a confusing or even humorous mental picture, like this: "I counted six squirrels riding my bike through the park that afternoon." Are the squirrels riding the bike? Probably not!

Practice: In the following correctly structured sentences, underline each participle or participial phrase and draw an arrow connecting it to its subject.

1. I never watch a game without my lucky charm, a hat worn by my grandfather.

2. We were amazed to see the musician playing guitar and harmonica at the same time.

3. The coughing boy breathed more easily as he was carried from the extinguished fire.

4. Singing along as security carried her away, the deranged fan blew kisses at the band.

5. The young architect imagining a building of impossible proportions was unable to find investors willing to support his dream.

6. The old man leaned against the wall next to the gate, his white mustache quivering a little as he snored.

Rewrite the following sentences so that each participle or participial phrase is correctly placed.

7. Rocking from side to side, the waves crashed against the small fishing boat.

8. The flower show was best known for its orchids, widely attended every year.

9. That new detective show supposedly has great writers premiering this fall.

10. Bowing under his weight, the man sat in a flimsy lawn chair.

11. The hermit was actually glad to see his hairstylist niece, bearded after months of solitude.

Answers:

1. "worn by my grandfather" → hat

2. "playing guitar and harmonica" → musician

3. coughing → boy; extinguished → fire

4. "singing along" → fan

5. "imagining a building" → architect; "willing to support his dream" → investors

6. quivering → mustache

(Suggested corrections)

7. The waves crashed against the small fishing boat rocking from side to side.

8. The flower show, widely attended every year, was best known for its orchids.

9. That new detective show premiering this fall supposedly has great writers.

10. The man sat in a flimsy lawn chair bowing under his weight.

11. Bearded after months of solitude, the hermit was actually glad to see his hairstylist niece.

Pronouns

The authors hope that the student reading *The New SAT Handbook* will find the pronouns section to be helpful. The authors have tried to keep the pronouns section concise and clear for the student reading *The New SAT Handbook*, because the authors realize that pronouns can be confusing—

Yikes, did that paragraph sound unnecessarily formal and wordy? Try it like this:

> *We* hope that *you* will find the section on pronouns to be helpful. *We* have tried to keep *it* concise and clear for *you*, because *we* realize that *they* can be confusing.

Pronouns can have a huge effect on how sentences sound and function. Pronouns are used in place of nouns to simplify and often shorten sentences. However, if used incorrectly, pronouns can create ambiguity (confusion). The most commonly tested types of pronouns are subjective, objective, and possessive.

Rule 1: A *subjective pronoun* is used to replace a noun serving as a *subject* within a sentence. Subjective pronouns include I, you, he, she, they, it, one, and we. You can identify a subjective pronoun the same way you would identify any subject: by matching it to a verb.

Examples: Nicole and *I* are going to the movie premiere tomorrow.

She talked to her parents, and *they* said that *we* must be back by midnight.

Did *you* know that Ameer said *he* could give us a ride home?

Rule 2: An *objective pronoun* is used to replace a noun serving as an *object* within a sentence. Objective pronouns include me, you, him, her, it, them, one, and us. Often an objective pronoun will follow a preposition, which is an automatic sign that it is replacing an object, not a subject.

Examples: Ameer might come with *us* to the premiere.

I have one extra ticket for *you*, *him*, or *her*.

If you want to use *it*, let *me* know right away so I can tell *them*.

Rule 3: A *possessive pronoun* is used to demonstrate ownership. Possessive pronouns include my/mine, your/yours, his, her/hers, their, its, and our/ours. Possessive pronouns can be used to show ownership of nouns and actions.

Examples: I gave *our* tickets to the usher; it was *his* job to help us find *our* seats.

"We appreciate *your* help," Ameer said to the usher and shook *his* hand.

I knew Mom and Dad appreciated *my* trying not to break curfew, even though I missed *their* deadline by five minutes.

Rule 4: A noun that is later replaced by a pronoun is called an *antecedent*; a pronoun must always be clearly "matchable" to its antecedent, and it must remain consistent in both person and number. "Person" refers to first-person (I/we), second-person (you), and third-person (he/she/they/one).

Examples: *Incorrect*: Danny and Connor were walking home when *he* realized *his* cell phone was still in *his* locker at school. *(Ambiguous whether the pronouns "he" and "his" refer to Danny or Connor.)*

Correct: Danny and Connor were walking home when ***Danny*** realized *his* cell phone was still in *his* locker at school. *(Danny is the clear antecedent for this sentence's pronouns.)*

Incorrect: If *one* wants to avoid losing a cell phone, *you* should enable the GPS. *(Switches from third-person "one" to second-person "you.")*

Correct: If *you* want to avoid losing a cell phone, *you* should enable the GPS. *(Pronouns are consistent in person.)*

Historically* Incorrect: If a museum visitor has questions, *they* should ask a docent. *("Visitor" is singular and "they" is a plural pronoun.)*

Correct: If a museum visitor has questions, *he* or *she* should ask a docent. *(Singular pronouns "he" and "she" match the singular "visitor.")*

*Please Note: In 2016, the Oxford English Dictionary revised its standards to accept "they" as a singular third-person pronoun. This change was made in response to contemporary cultural discussions of gender neutrality. Though this won't be a concern on the SAT, it is good scholarly information to have. And we've left this example here so that you can see the evolution of the English language, right before your eyes!

Rule 5: (Yes, there's a Rule 5. Pronouns have a lot of details!) Commonly confused pronouns include your/you're, their/they're/there, and its/it's. Just to review: ***Your***, ***their***, and ***its*** are all possessive pronouns. ***You're***, ***they're***, and ***it's*** are contractions of "you are," "they are," and "it is," respectively—all verb phrases with subjective pronouns. ***There*** is a unique word that can be used in a number of ways, but it is only a pronoun when it is replacing a place or concept.

If you're unsure which form of these commonly mixed-up words to use, ask yourself whether the word is showing ownership or representing an action.

Examples: If ***you're*** looking for a pen, you should check ***your*** desk.

That pen works fine; ***it's*** just missing ***its*** cap.

Acme Pen Company guarantees that its pens will work even if they lose ***their*** caps, because ***they're*** made with unique ink. You can see the guarantee right ***there*** on the label.

Cecil's Tips to Stay Sharp

Other pronoun types include demonstrative, reflexive, relative, interrogative, indefinite, and intensive. Yikes! For brief definitions of these less commonly tested pronouns, refer to the Grammar and Style Glossary beginning on page 48.

Practice: In the following sentences, fill in the correct pronoun for each blank.

1. I invited the Turners to come to the neighborhood picnic with Eric and ____ (I/me).

2. Curtis told me ____ (he/him) and his father are bringing their famous cole slaw.

3. Mrs. Turner said that she really appreciated ____ (our/us) inviting them.

4. "I have to get a copy of ____ (your/you're) cole slaw recipe!" she said.

5. Curtis's father smiled and said, "___ (It's/Its) a family secret, but I'll see what I can do."

6. I asked Curtis and Ray to join my team for volleyball, and ___ (he/they) said yes.

7. "If we're going to play, ____ (we/it) better start now," Ray said. "It's getting dark."

In the following sentences, circle all subjective, objective, and possessive pronouns and correct as needed.

8. The volleyball game was close; it was a tie until me and Ray scored two points.

9. After the game we went to a movie with Leah and Jayna; it was there treat because we won.

10. Leah and Jayna wanted to see a comedy, and since she was paying we agreed.

11. Curtis secretly wanted to see a drama but asked me to keep that between he and I.

12. For some reason Curtis insisted on buying my popcorn and soda.

13. Jayna shared her sour candies with Leah and us, saying "Its too sour for me!"

Answers:

1. Me
2. He
3. Our
4. Your
5. It's
6. They
7. We

8. It; me; "me" should be "I"
9. We; it; there; we; "there" should be "their"
10. She; we; "she" is ambiguous and should be changed to either "Jayna was," "Leah was," or "they were" if both were paying
11. Me; he; I; "he and I" should be "him and me"
12. My; no error
13. Her; us; its; me; "Its" should be "It's"… or "They're" would be even better, since "candies" is plural

Noun and Subject-Verb Agreement

The word "agreement" typically means a consensus of opinion (as in, "Both sides had reached an agreement"), but it also means a match between or among parts of speech. Remember, the test is focused on making sure that elements match within sentences. The two types of agreement to watch for are ***noun agreement*** and ***subject-verb agreement***.

Rule 1: ***Noun agreement*** (sometimes called noun-noun agreement) means that in a given sentence, all nouns that "go together" or refer to one another need to match in number. To check this, start with the subject of the sentence or clause and determine whether it is singular or plural. Then check any other nouns in the sentence that pertain to the subject to make sure that they match in number.

Examples: ***Incorrect***: Mr. Trainor reminded us that ***we*** needed to bring ***a sack lunch*** for the field trip. *("We" is plural, but "a sack lunch" is singular)*

Correct: Mr. Trainor reminded us that ***we*** needed to bring ***sack lunches*** for the field trip. *(Both nouns are plural)*

Incorrect: ***Washing*** dishes is my least favorite ***chores***. *("Washing" is a singular action, even though "dishes" is plural)*

Correct: ***Washing*** dishes is my least favorite ***chore***. *(Both are singular)*

Rule 2: ***Subject-verb agreement*** means that subjects should match their verbs in ***person*** (i.e., I, you, we, they, etc.) and ***number*** (singular or plural). The sentence's ***subject*** (the noun doing the action) determines the person and number of the verb; the sentence's ***object*** doesn't matter. To check this issue, identify either part and then match it to the other.

The subject does not always appear before the verb! Also, many words (often prepositional phrases) may separate the subject from the verb; they don't affect the subject-verb relationship. A safe rule is that if a noun follows a preposition, it's not the subject.

Examples: My ***dad sets*** the garbage cans on the curb every Monday night. *(Subject: dad; verb: sets)*

The garbage ***collectors*** with their loud truck ***wake*** me up every Tuesday morning. *(Subject: collectors; verb: wake)*

So loud ***are*** the ***gears*** of the garbage truck that my ***eyes pop*** open. *(Subject 1: gears; verb 1: are; subject 2: eyes; verb 2: pop)*

Rule 3: Several common subjects are tricky in terms of the numbers they represent. All of these words are *singular* subjects: anybody/anyone/anything, either, everybody/everyone/everything, neither, nobody/no one/nothing, somebody/someone/something. Words that refer to a single group (e.g., bunch, crowd, family, flock, group) are also singular.

Some *exceptional words*, like these, are also singular: alumna, alumnus, criterion, datum, medium, phenomenon, syllabus. Their plural forms, respectively, are: alumnae, alumni, criteria, data, media, phenomena, syllabi.

Also, some *other* words create a singular or plural based on the noun they belong with: all (of), none (of), any (of), some (of), and so on. This is sort of an exception to that rule of thumb given above about subjects not following prepositions; in a case like this, the word before the preposition is still the subject, but it's determined by what it belongs with.

Examples: I knocked, hoping *either* of the twins *was* home, but *nobody answered* the door.

Our research *group is* glad to receive new *data* that *support* the original hypothesis.

Some of the sandwiches *were* already missing from the buffet when I arrived.

Some of Uma's free time at camp *was* spent at the pool.

Rule 4: "And" is the *only* conjunction that joins two subjects to create a plural. Any other conjunction or joining phrase (or, but, along with, as well as, in addition to, etc.) cannot create a plural.

Examples: *Either* Patrick *or* Dominic *was* going to meet me after school.

Patrick *and* Dominic *were* going to meet me after school.

Monica *along with* Cory *needs* to submit her part of the group project.

Neither the butcher *nor* the baker *has* any idea where the candlestick maker went.

Practice: In the following sentences, draw an arrow from each subject to its verb.

1. My mother's company offered her a raise, and she took it gladly.

2. Paul has studied tirelessly for his history exam; other students have called it a nightmare.

3. The troupe of ballet dancers amazed us with its unique choreography.

4. So awestruck were we by the Grand Canyon that we completely forgot to take pictures.

5. One of the hardest things about standardized tests is the many topics they cover.

6. How should I choose the cell phone plan that is right for me?

In each of the following sentences, correct any noun or subject-verb agreement errors as needed. Some sentences may be correct as written.

7. Half the students in the class has never failed a test or quiz.

8. Mozart's *Requiem*, one of the most famous of all his compositions, were never finished.

9. A quality specialist checks to make sure all the jam jars leaving the factory have a label.

10. None of the fried chicken were eaten by the Olsens, who is a vegetarian.

11. In my opinion the finest painters of the Impressionist era were Monet and Cezanne.

12. The astronomers watch for comets, meteor showers, and other phenomenon.

Answers:

1. company → offered; she → took

2. Paul → has; students → have

3. troupe → amazed

4. we → were; we → forgot

5. one → is; they (pronoun for "tests") → cover

6. I → should; that (pronoun for "plan") → is

7. Half the students in the class *have* never failed a test or quiz.

8. Mozart's *Requiem*, one of the most famous of all his compositions, *was* never finished.

9. A quality specialist checks to make sure all the jam jars leaving the factory have *labels*.

10. None of the fried chicken *was* eaten by the Olsens, who *are vegetarians*.

11. Correct as written.

12. The astronomers watch for comets, meteor showers, and other *phenomena*.

Verb Tenses

Verbs are the powerhouses of sentences. They provide readers and listeners with actions and states of being. Verbs also provide context through ***conjugation*** (modification), both by matching their subjects in person and number and by telling us *when* actions or states occurred. Matching subjects and verbs was discussed in the previous module; this module focuses on tense, which provides the "when" of a verb.

For instance, these two sentences convey different information, don't they?

> *By the time the bell **rang**, we **had gotten** settled in our seats.*
>
> *By the time the bell **rings**, we **will have gotten** settled in our seats.*

One is set in the past and one is set in the future, and only verbs make the difference. In the English language there are many different tenses of verbs, but the SAT is chiefly concerned with two groups of three tenses each: the ***simple*** tenses and the ***perfect*** tenses. In the interest of more thorough preparation, we've included an additional group that is useful to understand and apply, both on and off the test: the ***continuous*** tenses.

Rule 1: The simple tenses are used to indicate past, present, and future actions and states. The ***simple past tense***, appropriately, describes an action or state that occurred in the past: "I went," "we saw," "they ate," etc.

The ***simple present tense*** describes an action or state that occurs in the moment: "I go," "we see," "they eat," etc.

The ***simple future tense*** describes an action or state that will occur in the future: "I will go," "we will see," "they will eat," etc. Unlike the other two, the simple future tense requires an ***auxiliary verb*** (or "helping" verb).

Examples: *This breed of orchid **is** difficult to find; it **was** previously believed to be extinct.*

*I **need** to check my schedule, and then I **will let** you know if I **can** attend.*

*The public library **closes** early on Saturdays.*

Cecil's Tips to Stay Sharp

Have you studied a language other than English? If so, good for you! In addition to expanding your horizons, you've simultaneously boosted your understanding of English grammar, especially verbs. Conjugation rules you might have learned in Spanish or French, about things like subjunctive and conditional moods and imperfect tenses, can also be applied to their English counterparts.

Rule 2: The perfect tenses are used to place actions and states in time relative to other things. The *past perfect tense* is used for actions and states that occurred earlier in time than other past events; this tense is composed of an auxiliary verb ("had") paired with the main verb's *past participle*: "I had *gone*," "we had *seen*," "they had *eaten*," etc.

The *present perfect tense* is used for actions and states that began in the past and continue into the present. This tense also requires an auxiliary verb ("have") and the main verb's past participle: "I have gone," "we have seen," "they have eaten," etc.

The *future perfect tense* is used for actions and states that will have occurred at some point in the future. This tense requires *two* auxiliary verbs ("will" and "have") joined by the past participle: "I will have gone," "we will have seen," "they will have eaten," etc.

Examples: *Charles Dickens **had attempted** a career in theatre before he began writing.*

*Identity theft **has become** a much bigger concern in recent years.*

*My plane **will have landed** by eight o'clock; I'll call as soon as I can.*

Rule 3: The continuous tenses are used to show actions or states that carry on without specified beginnings and endings; a continuous tense often offsets another main action within a sentence. Continuous tenses use the appropriate form of the auxiliary verb "be" followed by the *gerund* (-ing) form of the main verb. Any of the verb tenses described in Rules 1 and 2 can also be made into continuous tenses.

Examples: *Karen **was running** to the bus stop when her bus zoomed past. (past simple continuous)*

*We **are hoping** that you will consider our job offer. (present simple continuous)*

*Since I started that new migraine medication, I **have been feeling** much better. (present perfect continuous)*

Practice: In the following sentences, identify the tense of each underlined verb.

1. My father <u>is</u> an avid Tigers fan; he <u>has been</u> ever since they <u>won</u> the title in 1996.

2. Some early theorists <u>posited</u> that dinosaurs and humans <u>had coexisted</u> at some point.

3. I <u>called</u> ahead to let the tour group know that we <u>will be arriving</u> late.

4. Snowdrops <u>are</u> so hardy that they <u>bloom</u> earlier than almost any other spring flowers.

5. Bill <u>told</u> us all about the trip he <u>had taken</u> to Germany last summer.

6. You <u>are dreaming</u> if you <u>think</u> that you <u>will be</u> allowed out of the house in that shirt.

In each of the following sentences, correct any errors in verb tense as needed. Some sentences may be correct as written.

7. Josh went to school ever since he has turned three years old.

8. Paul Revere took his legendary midnight ride in 1776 to let the colonists know that the British are coming.

9. For the last decade, the poker tournament will be our most popular annual event.

10. Please let me know before you are leaving for the grocery store.

11. She did well on our last test, but she is feeling apprehensive about the next one.

12. By the time you leave this yoga class, you will have been feeling much more relaxed.

13. Adult coloring books became very popular last year; only time will tell if they will be remaining popular.

Answers:

1. is → present simple; has been → present perfect; won → past simple

2. posited → past simple; had coexisted → past perfect

3. called → past simple; will be arriving → future simple continuous

4. are → present simple; bloom → present simple

5. told → past simple; had taken → past perfect

6. are dreaming → present simple continuous; think → present simple; will be → future simple

7. Josh *has gone* to school ever since he *turned* three years old.

8. Paul Revere took his legendary midnight ride in 1776 to let the colonists know that the British *were* coming.

9. For the last decade, the poker tournament *has been* our most popular annual event.

10. Please let me know before you *leave* for the grocery store.

11. Correct as written

12. By the time you leave this yoga class, you *will be feeling/will feel* much more relaxed.

13. Adult coloring books became very popular last year; only time will tell if they *will remain* popular.

Word Choice and Idioms

Up to this point in the grammar and style review, things have been systematic; with occasional exceptions, everything has rules that you can follow to speak and write correctly.

Well, that ends here.

The two topics in this module—*word choice* and *idiomatic expressions*—have no set rules. The former refers to using the "right" word in a sentence (such as "effect" versus "affect"), and the latter are quirks of the English language that have evolved over centuries. They are like umbrellas brimming with exceptions. So how can you study them?

Before you abandon your grammar studies in disgust and dismay, hang on. There *are* a few rules (more like guidelines) that you can follow to catch potential errors on the test.

Rule 1: Errors in *word choice* (also known as *diction*) do not show up that often on the SAT, but they are useful to recognize in your own writing as well; for instance, if you used "except" instead of "accept" in your SAT essay, that error would affect the clarity and flow of your composition.

If you struggle with homophones like "weather"/"whether" and with similarly spelled words like "perpetrate"/"perpetuate," then the best study strategy is to "up" your reading game. Try to read more academic and critical content on a regular basis. Publications such as *The New York Times* and *The Wall Street Journal*, classic novels and novellas, and even professionally written movie reviews are all solid sources of reading practice.

After all, wouldn't you lift weights if you wanted to get stronger, or stretch if you wanted to become more flexible? It might sound like a big investment of time, but even ten minutes of challenging material per day will make you a stronger reader for life. That's well worth your time! Also, the more you read, the more likely you will catch errors like these wherever they pop up.

Examples: Fans of Smith's last novel will be delighted to pick up the illustrated *addition*. *(The word **addition** is incorrect; the correct term here is **edition**.)*

Following the discovery of penicillin, far fewer people have been *inflicted* with polio. *(**Inflicted** means having forced harm, which is close but incorrect; the proper term is **afflicted**, which means having caused suffering.)*

The lengthy seminar was so dull that it seemed *indeterminate*. *(If the emphasis is on length and dullness, then **interminable**, or endless, is the correct word.)*

Rule 2: Some word choice errors are due to words that sound alike, but others are due to errors of *number*. These errors can occur through mix-ups of *singular* and *plural* nouns (also known as *mass* and *count* nouns, respectively). These are more systematic than other word choice errors, so you can handle them by assessing the noun they describe.

If the noun is singular (e.g., coffee, sand, kindness), then it should be described with *little*, *less*, *least*, *much*, *more*, *most* or *amount*.

If the noun is plural (e.g., cups of coffee, grains of sand, acts of kindness), then it should be described with *few*, *fewer*, *fewest*, *many*, *more*, *most*, or *number*.

Greater is typically used in place of *more* to make comparisons of degree.

The exceptions to the singular-plural noun rule are *time*, *money*, *distance*, and *weight*. Even though they are measured in plural units (minutes, dollars, etc.), amounts or spans of them are considered singular.

Examples: How **much** coffee and donuts have you had? *(**Coffee** is singular, so **much** is correct, but **donuts** are plural and should be described by "how **many**.")*

Sometimes I sneak into the "ten items or **less**" checkout lane with eleven items. *(Incorrect: **Items** are plural, so the correct phrase is "ten items or **fewer**.")*

How **many** hours have you been standing in line? *(**Many** is correct because the hours in line are plural, meaning they can be counted.)*

I have spent **more** than six hours waiting in this line for tickets! *(Correct: **Six hours** is a singular span of time here, but it is **more** either way.)*

Rule 3: An *idiom* or idiomatic expression is an accepted way of expressing something within a linguistic culture. Idioms can be *colloquial* or *figurative expressions*, such as "to break up with someone" and "on the edge of his seat," or they can be *prepositional* and *gerund/infinitive* idioms, such as the difference between "to agree upon" and "agreeing with."

The SAT only tests prepositional and gerund/infinitive idioms. To native English speakers and people who read frequently, errors in these types of idioms often "just sound wrong."

If you think that you're looking at an idiom error—if something in a sentence "just sounds wrong"—then **check any prepositions and verbs in that sentence**. For each one ask yourself, "Can I think what preposition or verb would make more sense here?" Idioms rely upon your reading "ear" and your ability to trust yourself when something seems off. Go with your gut!

Examples: After their kids leave *to* college, many parents decide traveling more. *(The preposition **to** should be **for**; the gerund **traveling** should be the infinitive **to travel**.)*

After their children go *to* college, many parents consider *traveling* more. *(This one is correct as it is, even with the preposition and gerund that didn't fit before.)*

Some reality show contestants seem to be there solely *for the creating of* drama. *(The gerund phrase **for the creating of** should be the infinitive **to create**.)*

Practice: In each of the following sentences, consider the underlined words and expressions. Correct any idiom or word choice errors as needed. (Remember, these errors often "just sound wrong.") Some sentences may be correct as written.

1. <u>Of all the stores</u> with Black Friday sales, that store has the most <u>incredulous</u> deals. [incredible]

2. The armed forces of our country strive <u>to defend against</u> threats and attacks. [C]

3. This candidate, first <u>regarded to be</u> [as] an unlikely contender, is now <u>leading up</u> [in] the polls.

4. The <u>principle</u> [principal] witness for the prosecution gave a great <u>amount</u> [number] of convincing pieces of evidence of the man's guilt.

5. However, the defendant provided an alibi that was <u>inconsistent to</u> [with] the witness's story.

6. Tara bargained hard for her new car and <u>ended up</u> paying almost a thousand <u>dollars fewer</u> [less] than the dealer's alleged "lowest" offer.

7. High school students need <u>less high-stakes tests</u> [fewer] and <u>more emphasis</u> [greater] on core concepts.

8. The young man was clearly nervous; I could hear his voice <u>waiver</u> [waver] when he spoke.

9. Children have loved fairy tales <u>from</u> [for] generations, not realizing their darker <u>illusions</u>. [allusion]

10. I could not forget <u>calling back</u> [to call] the insurance agent before the end of the business day.

11. We were relieved when volunteers <u>began arriving</u> [to arrive] in <u>greater numbers</u> than before.

12. This week the farmers market <u>plans including</u> [include] fresh strawberries, asparagus, and <u>much</u> [many] varieties of lettuce.

Answers:

1. "Of all the stores" is correct; "incredulous" should be "incredible."

2. Correct as written

3. "Regarded to be" should be "considered to be" or "regarded as"; "leading up" should be "leading in."

4. "Principle" should be "principal"; "amount of convincing pieces of evidence" should either be "amount of convincing evidence" or "number of convincing pieces of evidence."

5. "Inconsistent to" should be "inconsistent with."

6. "Ended up" is correct; "dollars fewer" should be "dollars less."

7. "Less high-stakes tests" should be "fewer high-stakes tests"; "more emphasis" should be "greater emphasis."

8. "Waiver" should be "waver."

9. "From" should be "for"; "illusions" should be "allusions."

10. "Calling back" should be "to call back."

11. Correct as written

12. "Plans including" should be "plans to include"; "much" should be "many."

Common Punctuation Issues

Judging from things we've read online and in print, an awful lot of people are awfully confused about punctuation. All those little lines and dots and squiggles have different functions, so we're going to clear up some of the confusion with a brief punctuation guide you can use for the SAT—and for any other writing you do anytime, anywhere, ever.

Marks that End Sentences

There are three punctuation marks that end sentences: the *period* (.), the *question mark* (?), and the *exclamation mark* (!).

The *period* is the basic sentence-ending mark you should use most of the time. The period says, "We have now come to the end of a complete thought."

> *Today we will go swimming in the ocean.*
> *"I hope we don't see any sharks," Amber said.*

Cecil's Tips to Stay Sharp

Detail-oriented readers might notice a fair number of exclamation marks throughout this guide. They are meant to be encouraging as you work through the explanations for concepts and practice problems. We shout because we care!

The *question mark* should be used at the end of a question. You should use it when the sentence itself is a question, and you should also use it when the sentence reports that someone is asking a question.

> *Have you ever seen a shark in the wild?*
> *Nick asked, "Isn't that a shark fin out there?"*

The *exclamation mark* (sometimes called an exclamation point) indicates excitement, urgency, or surprise. Exclamation marks are useful in reported speech.

> *"Shark!" Jessie shouted. "Get out of the water!"*

You should avoid using exclamation marks elsewhere in your writing, however. Using unnecessary exclamation marks to grab the reader's attention can often backfire, because it reads like the writer is shouting. On the SAT, and in other writing you do, let each idea speak for itself without "shouting."

Marks that Let You Quote People

As you probably know, **quotation marks** ("") are used to set apart statements from other sources, both for dialogue or quotes and for research citations. You probably also know that you're supposed to introduce or close a quote with a comma most of the time. Here are a couple of examples:

> *Joyce asked, "What's the big deal about sharks?"*
> *"Ask my cousin Lefty," Jeff replied.*

So far, so good, right? However, there are exceptions. For example, if a quote ends with a question mark or an exclamation mark, you wouldn't follow it with a comma.

> *"Is that a dead jellyfish?" Vladi asked.*
> *"Eww!" squeaked Rebecca.*

You also shouldn't use a comma if you're splicing together your words and someone else's to express a complete thought—for instance, when you're researching something or quoting a source of information.

> ***Incorrect****: This book says that sharks are, "dangerous to anything that looks tasty."*
> ***Correct****: This book says that sharks are "dangerous to anything that looks tasty."*
> ***Also Correct****: This book says, "Sharks are dangerous to anything that looks tasty."*

You also shouldn't use a comma if you're giving the name of a general term, or if you want to imply that a term is untrustworthy.

> *The book also says that sharks' jaws are called "death chompers."*
> *Where is this author getting these "facts" about sharks, anyhow?*

Finally, there's the question of whether punctuation at the end of a quote should go inside or outside the quotation marks. Sometimes the matter is clear. For example, if a sentence asks a question and ends in a quotation, but the quotation is not itself a question, the question mark goes outside the quotation marks.

> *Does the author really think sharks are "the garbage disposals of the sea"?*

The debate centers on smaller marks, especially periods and commas. American writers tend to argue that putting periods and commas inside the quotation marks gives the sentence a more aesthetically pleasing look.

On the cover, the author calls herself a "Professional Sharkologist."

British writers, however, prefer to put the periods and commas inside the quotation marks only if they are part of the material that is quoted; otherwise, they put the periods and commas outside the quotation marks.

Somehow I doubt that her actual title is "Sharkologist".

On the SAT, and in any other context where a teacher or supervisor says so, you're better off following the American convention. In other writing you do, you may be free to choose, but you should be consistent within a given story, essay, or other document.

Marks that Interrupt Sentences

Sometimes a sentence will be interrupted by another thought called an ***appositive***. An appositive isn't usually a complete sentence by itself; rather, it supplies additional information to supplement the sentence it interrupts. If the appositive is removed, what remains is still a complete, grammatically correct sentence.

An appositive is set off by two matching punctuation marks, one on either end, that must both be present in order for the appositive to be correct. You can think of them like bookends that must both be present in order to keep the books from falling over.

There are three pairs of punctuation marks that can be used to set off an appositive: ***commas*** (, ,), ***em dashes*** (— —), and ***parentheses*** (( )).

How do you choose which punctuation to use? Generally, commas provide the smallest degree of interruption. Em dashes provide the greatest degree of interruption, so they're useful if you want the interruption to feel a little jarring. Parentheses are somewhere in the middle.

None of us (as far as I can remember) had ever seen a shark in the wild.
Even Liz, who had been a champion swimmer in college, did not brave the waters.
Nothing—except a shark—could have kept her out of the water.

Sometimes people treat an identifying word or phrase as an appositive when it really shouldn't be one. This happens especially when the appositive is someone's name.

> *Incorrect*: *My dad's friend, Richard, was nearly attacked by a shark once.*
> *Correct*: *My dad's friend Richard was nearly attacked by a shark once.*

This isn't an appositive because the father presumably has more than one friend, so we need the name to follow it. But note that if you start with the name, an explanation of who or what the name belongs to *is* an appositive. That's because the explanation provides useful additional information, but you don't actually need it in order to correctly identify the person you're talking about.

> *Incorrect*: *Tori Richard's wife rolls her eyes when he tells his shark attack story.*
> *Correct*: *Tori, Richard's wife, rolls her eyes when he tells his shark attack story.*

Without the appositive "Richard's wife" in this sentence, we don't know that Tori and Richard's wife are the same person, but we can identify the main action without it (Tori rolls her eyes).

So how do you know when to treat an identifying word or phrase as an appositive and when not to? If you can remove the identifying word or phrase without changing the overall meaning of the sentence, then treat it as an appositive. If removing the word or phrase would take away from the clarity or meaning of the sentence, then it shouldn't be an appositive.

Marks that Relate Ideas in Sentences

Punctuation marks can shape sentences in other ways as well, especially by showing the relationships between ideas. The marks that serve this purpose include *em dashes* (—), *colons* (:), *semicolons* (;), and *commas* (,).

We saw *em dashes* earlier when we talked about appositives, because one way to set off an appositive is to put an em dash on either end of it. One em dash by itself has any of a few different functions in the sentence, however.

One function is to transition from one idea to the next with a sharper break than a comma would provide, as though the new idea is a surprise or an interruption.

> *We stood on the beach and watched the waves—until the tide came in, that is.*

Another function of the em dash is to relate the part of the sentence that comes before it to the part of the sentence that comes after it. The em dash refers the reader backward from the later part to the earlier part.

> *"Sharks—they give me the willies," Simon commented.*

A ***colon*** can also be used to relate the first and second parts of a sentence; however, the colon refers the reader forward from the earlier part to the later part.

> *Trish declared, "There are only two things I'm afraid of: sharks and drowning."*

In this sentence, the colon introduces a list. The word "things" before the colon points forward across the colon to the list that enumerates what the "things" are.

If you're going to use a colon to introduce a list, make sure that the part of the sentence before the colon contains a noun or pronoun that refers to the items in the list. You should also avoid using words like "like" or "such as" if you're using a colon. For example:

> **Correct**: *The sign on the beach warned of three dangers: sharks, jellyfish, and riptides.*
> **Incorrect**: *The sign warned of: sharks, jellyfish, and riptides.*
> **Also Incorrect**: *The sign warned of dangers such as: sharks, jellyfish, and riptides.*

If you can remove the colon and still have a grammatically correct sentence, then the colon doesn't belong in the sentence in the first place and you should leave it out. If removing the colon leaves you with a sentence that doesn't quite work correctly, then the colon is doing important work and you should put it back where you found it.

The ***semicolon*** is an odd little mark that looks like a regular colon got a comma stuck to its foot. A semicolon has two and only two functions.

One function of a semicolon is to separate items in a list when at least one item in that list already has a comma in it. This function is sometimes necessary for clarity.

> **Unclear (with only commas)**: *The Baltic States' capitals are Tallinn, Estonia, Riga, Latvia, and Vilnius, Lithuania.*
> **Clear (with semicolons)**: *The Baltic States' capitals are Tallinn, Estonia**;** Riga, Latvia**;** and Vilnius, Lithuania.*

The other function of a semicolon is to join two independent clauses into one sentence without using a conjunction. You might use a semicolon this way if you want to show that the two clauses are closely related without using a conjunction to state precisely how they're related.

> *The Baltic States have nothing to do with sharks; they're just a convenient example.*

A semicolon can also be used to correct a run-on sentence; refer to the grammar exercise on page 56 if you'd like more practice with this topic.

And that's it! Semicolons really aren't that scary.

Finally, we come to the **comma**. As we've mentioned, commas are useful when you want a sentence to include a quotation or an appositive. Commas can also help you connect or separate ideas.

Cecil's Tips to Stay Sharp

You probably already learned in school that commas can separate items in a list. That's correct.

> *The sharks we saw included nurse sharks, lemon sharks, and a tiger shark.*

You probably also learned about commas and conjunctions in school. Judging from some of the writing we've seen, though, a lot of people have the wrong idea about commas and conjunctions. Putting a comma in front of a **coordinating conjunction** (for, and, nor, but, or, yet, so) is often required.

> *I had never been to the ocean, so I was disappointed that I couldn't go swimming.*

Putting a comma after a conjunction, however, is almost never correct.

> **Incorrect**: *A few of us walked along the beach, and, we found some interesting seashells.*

The comma before the last item in a list is called the "serial comma" or "Oxford comma." Use of the serial comma varies widely from one discipline to the next; for example, it is not used in journalism, but it is used in research writing. We recommend using it because it clarifies that the last two items in a list are separate items.

You don't always need a comma in front of a conjunction, however. For example, when you are creating a list of only two items, the conjunction by itself is enough.

The shark platter comes with coleslaw and hush puppies.

If you'd like to review the use of conjunctions, check out the grammar modules beginning on pages 53 and 58.

Another place people like to put commas but shouldn't is immediately after the subject of a sentence:

Incorrect: *Our server, brought out the food on steaming plates.*

Appositives, however, are the exception to any rule about where commas don't belong. If you're inserting an appositive somewhere and you're bookending that appositive with commas, use those commas.

Correct: *We walked along the beach and, to our surprise, we found some interesting seashells.*
Correct: *Our server, whose name was Matt, brought out the food on steaming plates.*

You should sometimes use commas in **compound sentences**, which are sentences formed from multiple independent clauses that are linked with conjunctions. So how do you know when to use them? One good rule of thumb is that, if you're linking clauses with different subjects or if you're linking more than two clauses, you should use commas. You might also want to use commas if you are showing contrast or if one clause describes a state while another describes an action. Here are some examples:

Bobby was hungry, but he chewed slowly so he didn't choke on any fish bones.
  (The first clause is a state; the second is an action.)
Some members of the group ordered dessert, and they ate it with gusto.
  (The first clause uses the noun "members"; the second uses a pronoun in its place.)
After dinner we stood up and stretched, we piled back into our cars, and we drove home.
  (There are three clauses here.)

If clauses are linked with **subordinating conjunctions** (after, because, before, since, etc.), a comma must be used if the subordinating conjunction begins the sentence. This is not necessarily the case if the subordinating conjunction comes after the first clause.

> ***Correct***: *Though the snow continued to fall, the school district did not cancel school.*
> ***Also Correct***: *I hurried to finish my online assignment because it was due by midnight.*
> ***Also Correct***: *Because my online assignment was due by midnight, I hurried to finish it.*

A final use for commas is to set off a ***participle*** or participial phrase, usually one that functions like an adverb, from the rest of the sentence.

> *Tired as we were, we kept each other awake for the long drive.*
> *Creaking with sunburn, we lurched our way out of the car and up the stairs.*

Marks that Unite or Break Up Words

Some punctuation marks go between or inside words to bring them together, shorten them, or convey certain other information.

One such mark is the ***hyphen*** (-), which is shorter than the em dash discussed above. A hyphen goes between two words to tie them together. You might be familiar with this use of hyphens already if you or someone you know has a hyphenated last name. Hyphens should be used if the words they put together will function like an adjective or noun in the sentence; they should not be used if the words they join would function like a verb or adverb.

> *I like to visit my five-year-old nephew.*
> *He has a crush on a six-year-old.*
> *My nephew doesn't realize that he is only five years old.*

Some words take hyphens with certain prefixes, while other words would use those same prefixes without hyphens. "Non-" is an especially common prefix under this rule. For example:

> *Lianne enjoys nontraditional pizza toppings like shrimp and carrots.*
> *Amy has a non-confrontational personality, so she eats Lianne's pizzas without comment.*

We wish there were a hard-and-fast rule we could tell you to help you figure out which words are which, but there isn't one. We're just telling you this fact so you'll be able to keep your eye out for examples on your own.

Cecil's Tips to Stay Sharp

There are no such phrases as "should of," "would of," "might of," and so on. The actual phrases are "should have," "would have," and "might have," and their contracted forms are "should've," "would've," and "might've."

There's another mark that sometimes plays a role in uniting words, and that's the ***apostrophe*** ('). The apostrophe unites words when used as part of a ***contraction***. A contraction, in turn, is formed when two or more words are combined into one and some letters are replaced with an apostrophe. Here are some examples:

can not → can't
I would → I'd
might have → might've
we will → we'll
they are → they're
she has → she's
that is → that's
let us → let's

You should generally avoid using contractions in formal writing, like on the SAT Essay Test. Though they aren't grammatically wrong, they are often perceived as inappropriately casual.

Marks that Make Words Possessive

Apostrophes also get used to show that one person or thing possesses another. Usually you form the possessive by adding an apostrophe-s (**'s**) at the end of whatever thing possesses the other thing. If more than one thing possesses a thing, you put the apostrophe after the s (**s'**).

Did you sew Ralph's jacket's button back on?
    (The button belongs to the jacket; the jacket belongs to Ralph.)
We should figure out who's going to the kids' teachers' presentations.
    (There are multiple kids; each has a teacher who is giving a presentation.)

There are a few exceptions to this rule, however. Words with irregular plurals (that is, words that don't become plural by just tacking an -s onto the end) form the plural possessive by adding an apostrophe-s, just like singular words do:

In the women's dorm at my college there's a student from the People's Republic of China.

Probably the most commonly used (and misused) exception in possessives, the pronoun *it* forms the possessive without an apostrophe (probably because "it's" is already a contraction for "it is" or "it has"):

*It's been a long time since my car had **its** oil changed.*

Slightly less common but also commonly misunderstood, the possessive form of the pronoun *who* is "whose." ("Who's" is a contraction of "who is" or "who has.")

Whose boots did I trip over at the back door?

Finally, certain proper names that end in "s" can form the possessive either by adding an apostrophe-s or by adding an apostrophe without the extra "s" at the end:

Whose beard do you think is better: Moses', Jesus', or St. Francis'?
I'd rank them in this order, best to worst: Moses's, Jesus's, then St. Francis's.

Either form is acceptable, but the form without the extra "s" is more common. In any case, you should pick one and use it consistently throughout a given story, essay, or other piece of writing.

Marks that Make Words Plural

That's sort of a trick heading, because it's very, very rare to use punctuation marks when making words plural. One exception: If you're forming the plural of a single letter, especially if the letter is lowercase, the apostrophe-s pluralization is acceptable:

*Remember to dot your **i's** and cross your **t's**!*

If the letter is uppercase, however, leave out the apostrophe and use a lowercase "s":

*My brother's music is all on old-fashioned tapes and **CDs**.*

Do not use the apostrophe when forming the plurals of numbers, even if you write the numbers using numerals:

> **Correct**: *He has **100s** of CDs, most of which he bought in the **1990s**.*

Note that if you want to write the plural of a number like in that first example, you should just write out the word. "Hundreds" is more acceptable in formal writing than "100s." If you want to refer to a century or decade, however, the "1990s" form used in that sentence is fine.

Speaking of years, if you want to abbreviate a year or a decade, place an apostrophe in front of it to represent the missing digits, the same way you use an apostrophe to represent the missing letters in a contraction:

> *A lot of good music was made in the **'60s**, but my favorite album came out in **'74**.*

Marks that Stand In for Missing Words and Phrases

Remember the apostrophe that shows where letters are missing from a word? Sometimes you want to show that whole words or phrases are missing from a sentence, and for that, you need an ***ellipsis*** (...). Sometimes you also might need multiple ellipses (the plural form of ellipsis).

You will use the ellipsis most often when you want to quote something but you want to take some words out of the middle of your quotation. The ellipsis allows you to do that without having to quote each part separately.

> *Hamlet said, "To be, or not to be—that is the question: Whether 'tis nobler in the mind to suffer ... Or ... to die."*

Anyone well-versed in Shakespeare's play *Hamlet* will know that there are some words missing where the ellipses are.

You don't usually need an ellipsis at the beginning or end of a quotation, incidentally. Your readers can safely assume that your source says other things before and after the words you quoted; you only need to show them where you left words out in the middle.

Sometimes if you're writing dialogue, you might use an ellipsis in the middle of a sentence to show a pause or at the end of a sentence to show that a speaker was interrupted or that he or she trailed off without finishing a thought:

The detective declared, "The murderer is ... the butler!"
"He killed her," the detective continued, "because ..."

... Well, you'll just have to discern the butler's motive for yourself.

A final note

This is not a complete guide to all punctuation marks and their uses by any means, but it is a solid review of all the basics you'll need to write, read, and edit effectively on the new SAT. If you have additional questions, feel free to take them to your friendly neighborhood English teacher. We bet that he or she would be positively delighted by your keen interest in proper punctuation.

Read on for realistic Writing and Language Test practice sets!

Chapter 6: Writing and Language Practice Set

Here are some practice passages for the writing test, complete with grammar mistakes and other kinds of things you'll see on the SAT.

Fruits and Vegetables

Many people are familiar with the question of whether a tomato is a fruit or a vegetable. Botanists would say that it is a fruit, because it is a seed-bearing part of a plant that forms from a flower. Chefs, however, often think <u>₁</u> of tomatoes as vegetables because they taste savory rather than sweet. So who's right?

They both are. In culinary terms, the category of "fruit" includes any edible, sweet-tasting part of the plant, usually but not always seed-<u>bearing, the category of "vegetable"</u> ₂ includes any edible part of the plant that is not

1. (A) NO CHANGE
   (B) Chefs however, often think
   (C) Chefs, however often think
   (D) Chefs, however often, think

2. (A) NO CHANGE
   (B) bearing; also, the category of "vegetable"
   (C) bearing, however, the category of "vegetable"
   (D) bearing; the category of "vegetable," on the other hand,

especially sweet. In botanical terms, however, the category of "fruits" include parts ₃ formed from certain flower tissues and one or more ovaries, but the category of "vegetables" does not exist.

Botanically speaking, there is no such thing as "vegetables." ₄ Most of the foods we call "fruits" are true fruits in the botanical sense, and nearly all of them bear seeds in some way, or at least they would if they had not been bred into "seedless" varieties. The foods we call "vegetables," however, include leaves, stalks, roots, and other plant parts that have nothing in common except that they are parts of plants.

Why don't botanists and chefs just agree on a common set of categories so we don't have to wonder whether cucumbers, peppers, and gourds, should ₅ be called fruits or vegetables?

The reason is because botanists and chefs ₆ have different priorities. Botanists need to identify the anatomies of the plants they study with precision. When different kinds of plants each have parts that perform similar functions, like oranges and pumpkins do, botanists find it useful to group them into the same category, irregardless ₇ of what the parts look like or how they taste.

3. (A) NO CHANGE
   (B) "fruits" includes parts
   (C) "fruits" include a part
   (D) "fruits" includes a part

4. (A) NO CHANGE
   (B) is no such thing as a "vegetable."
   (C) is no such things as "vegetables."
   (D) is no such thing, as a "vegetable."

5. (A) NO CHANGE
   (B) gourds, they should
   (C) gourds should
   (D) gourds that should

6. (A) NO CHANGE
   (B) The reason being that botanists and chefs
   (C) Botanists and chefs disagree because they
   (D) Botanists disagree with chefs because they

7. (A) NO CHANGE
   (B) without regard to
   (C) regardlessly
   (D) regardless

Chefs, on the other hand, are more concerned with the flavors, textures, and nutritional content ₈ of the foods they work with than they are with how those parts function in living plants. Even plants with similar anatomies can taste very different from each other, like oranges and pumpkins do, ₉ chefs find it useful to group those parts into different categories. Likewise, when parts that perform different roles for a different plant ₁₀ share certain flavor characteristics, like broccoli and spinach do, chefs find it useful to group those parts into the same category.

In addition to the importance of nutrition, then, the different ways botanists and chefs use the terms "fruit" and "vegetable" highlight the fluidity of language and the importance of context.

8. (A) NO CHANGE
(B) flavors, textural and nutritional content
(C) flavors textures and nutritional content
(D) flavors and textural, as well as nutritional content

9. (A) NO CHANGE
(B) like oranges and pumpkins do
(C) like oranges and pumpkins do, so
(D) for instance oranges and pumpkins,

10. (A) NO CHANGE
(B) for any individual plant
(C) differently for all plants
(D) for different plants

11. Which of the following would be most appropriate to add after the last sentence of the passage?
(A) A "fruit" in a laboratory could easily be considered a "vegetable" in a kitchen.
(B) Because of the importance of nutrition, chefs should be taken more seriously than botanists.
(C) That is why you can think of a tomato as both a vegetable and a fruit.
(D) Also, discussing fruits and vegetables in other languages would be still more complicated.

Science Fiction Literature

People who study "serious" literature sometimes look down upon science fiction. Science fiction, they say is [12] merely escapist storytelling which draws the reader's attention with imaginary creatures, technologies, and settings rather than stimulating the reader's intelligence with a character-driven meditation on some grand moral or philosophical theme.

By and large, however, this accusation is ill-founded. While no doubt there are some works of science fiction—and indeed of every genre—that exist purely to sell cheap paperbacks in an airport gift shop [14], quite a few works of science fiction deal with exactly the sort of themes those critics prize. Further, by setting their stories in imaginary lands and filling them with advanced technologies, science fiction stories [15] can explore their chosen themes from perspectives that would not be possible in stories set on a realistic Earth.

Take, for example, Frank Herbert's 1965 novel *Dune*. Set on a desert planet, *Dune* explores the interaction of the environment and human culture by

12. (A) NO CHANGE
    (B) Science fiction, they say, is
    (C) Science, fiction they say, is
    (D) Science fiction they say, is

13. The author's tone in the second paragraph is
    (A) outraged
    (B) sardonic
    (C) persuasive
    (D) hopeful

14. (A) NO CHANGE
    (B) in a gift shop in an airport
    (C) in airport gift shops
    (D) in airports and gift shops

15. (A) NO CHANGE
    (B) science fiction authors
    (C) science, fiction and stories
    (D) science fiction and authors

contrasting the ways the tribal Fremen adapt to life in the desert with the ways rulers from other planets try, at great expense, to maintain their accustomed lifestyles. Another of *Dune*'s major themes is politics, it contrasts ₁₆ the approaches different rulers take toward the Fremen and the resulting attitudes the Fremen develop toward those rulers.

The "what-if" aspect of science fiction allows authors to posit an idea or a scenario and explore its social ramifications. Neal Stephenson's 2008 novel *Anathem* asks ₁₇ what might happen to a society in which all the scientists, philosophers, and other advanced thinkers live in cloistered communities, cut off from the outside world—and what happens when the outside world suddenly needs their help.

Some works of science fiction anticipate and even drive real-world developments. William Gibson's 1984 novel *Neuromancer* may not have been the first work to predict that, in an era of interconnected computers, information theft will be ₁₈ a high-stakes form of crime, but it was one of the first to popularize the notion. *Neuromancer* also popularized the term "cyberspace," which Gibson himself had coined in a

16. (A) NO CHANGE
    (B) politics; it contrasts,
    (C) politics. It contrasted
    (D) politics; the novel contrasts

17. (A) NO CHANGE
    (B) novel *Anathem* is asking
    (C) novel *Anathem* had asked
    (D) novel *Anathem* will ask

18. (A) NO CHANGE
    (B) information theft has been
    (C) information theft is becoming
    (D) information theft would be

19. Which additional detail would most enhance the author's example of Gibson's novel *Neuromancer*?
    (A) *Neuromancer* has sold over 6.5 million copies worldwide.
    (B) The popular film franchise *The Matrix* was later inspired by *Neuromancer*.
    (C) Other authors have even posited that Gibson's writing helped to inspire the development of the World Wide Web.
    (D) After writing *Neuromancer*, Gibson wrote several other novels.

short story two years earlier and which has since come into widespread usage.

Influential people have begun noticing science fiction's popularity as well as it's impact [20] on the broader culture. The 1960s saw the first college-level courses and academic journals devoted to the study of science fiction. Since the 1990s, some colleges and universities have even been offering graduate-level degrees in science fiction studies. Civic leaders have also taken note of the millions of dollars that fans of science fiction spend at popular conventions held in cities around the country. At last, science fiction, seems [22] to be getting the respect many of its fans feel is overdue.

20. (A) NO CHANGE
 (B) its impact
 (C) their impacts
 (D) its impacting

21. Which of the following would most enhance the last paragraph?
 (A) A personal example of a convention attended by the author.
 (B) An example of a high-profile academic who studies science fiction.
 (C) An opposing argument against the study of science fiction that the author can then debunk.
 (D) An example of a civic leader who has acknowledged the funds raised by conventions.

22. (A) NO CHANGE
 (B) At last, science fiction, it seems
 (C) At last science, fiction seems
 (D) At last, science fiction seems

Sociology and Anthropology

To students of the social sciences, the difference between sociology and anthropology can seem arbitrary. Both disciplines center on the studying of people, 23 so why do they often constitute different departments at colleges and universities? Why are Sociology 101 and Anthropology 101 classes taught by different professors using different textbooks?

It turns out that there are indeed certain differences between sociology and anthropology that may account for their constituting 25 separate academic departments. One difference is that sociological research is often more quantitative while anthropologists study qualitative things 26. That is, sociologists do much of their research by conducting surveys and compiling statistics. Their main concern is with trends, correlations, and which types of people are thinking and doing what kinds of things. Their data is used for measuring of 27 those trends and correlations. Anthropologists, on the other hand, do much of their research by talking with people, observing people's actions, and looking at bones and artifacts. Their main concern is with the meanings and

23. (A) NO CHANGE
    (B) studies of people
    (C) study of people
    (D) studying of peoples

24. What compositional technique does the author use in the first paragraph to introduce the topic?
    (A) rhetorical questions
    (B) personal anecdotes
    (C) specific examples
    (D) expert opinions

25. (A) NO CHANGE
    (B) them constituting
    (C) they constitute
    (D) there constituting

26. (A) NO CHANGE
    (B) anthropological research studies things that are qualitative
    (C) anthropologists are more qualitative in their studies
    (D) anthropological studies are more qualitative

27. (A) NO CHANGE
    (B) They use data to measure
    (C) There data is used to measure
    (D) Their data are used in the measuring of

ideas that people associate <u>with actions, symbols, and with objects</u> ₂₈.

This distinction is not as sharp as it may appear, however. For example, in order to understand their statistics and survey results, <u>subjects in sociological studies often have to be interviewed</u> ₂₉ about how they perceive whatever factors the sociologists are studying. Anthropologists, meanwhile, often have to use statistical correlations to supplement their other data, such as to see whether the ways people act correspond to the things they say are important. Thus, sociologists and anthropologists both do quantitative and qualitative research, even if they balance those kinds of research in different ways.

Another difference people sometimes observe between sociology and anthropology is that <u>sociological research tends to happen in</u> ₃₀ North America and Europe, but anthropologists tend to research people in other parts of the world. In other words, there is a sense that sociologists study "us" and anthropologists study "them." <u>Fortunately,</u> ₃₁ there has often been some truth to this distinction. As researchers in both fields have become aware of it, however, they have begun

28. (A) NO CHANGE
    (B) with actions, symbols and objects
    (C) with actions, with symbols, and objects
    (D) with actions, symbols, and objects

29. (A) NO CHANGE
    (B) sociologists' study subjects often have to be interviewed by them
    (C) sociologists often have to interview their study subjects
    (D) sociologists often have to be interviewed by their study subjects

30. (A) NO CHANGE
    (B) sociologists tend to study people in
    (C) sociologists tend to be found researching in
    (D) sociological research tends to be conducted by researchers in

31. (A) NO CHANGE
    (B) On the other hand,
    (C) Regrettably,
    (D) Uncertainly,

changing the way they choose their research topics and the places they apply their research methods. Sociologists have begun conducting surveys and compiling statistics on societies other than their own, and anthropologists around the world has started to observe ₃₁ rituals and look with new eyes at the artifacts of their own cultures.

It is too soon to say whether the disciplines of sociology and anthropology will ever merge, because they do still emphasize different research methods and kinds of data. As both disciplines expand their scope to all humans everywhere, however, they are inching further from a study of "us" and "them" and closer to a study of humanity as a whole.

32. (A) NO CHANGE
    (B) has started observing
    (C) have started the observing of
    (D) have started to observe

33. The overall tone of this passage is
    (A) academic
    (B) patronizing
    (C) upbeat
    (D) sardonic

Writing and Language Practice Set Answers

1. A
2. D
3. B
4. B
5. C
6. C
7. D
8. A
9. C
10. D
11. A
12. B
13. C
14. C
15. B
16. D
17. A
18. D
19. C
20. B
21. B
22. D
23. C
24. A
25. A
26. D
27. B
28. D
29. C
30. B
31. C
32. D
33. A

Chapter 7: The Math Test

Overview

The previous chapters have focused on the verbal sections of the new SAT, but now it's time to dive into mathematics. Fear not! These chapters will review the structure of the Math section, teach helpful strategies to break down just about every question, and provide practice and content review for dozens of math concepts.

How will the test be set up?

The Math Test on the new SAT will be composed of two sections: one with a calculator and one with no calculator. The calculator section will have 30 multiple-choice questions and 8 student-produced response (grid-in) questions, to be completed within 55 minutes. The no-calculator section will be 25 minutes long, with 15 multiple-choice questions and 5 student-produced response questions.

Two questions in the calculator section will be an "extended thinking question set," worth double the raw points of the other questions. There will be no wrong-answer penalty on the new SAT, including any of the Math questions, so you should never leave anything blank!

What sort of content will be tested? How should I prepare?

The College Board has identified four overall topics for the Math Test: "Heart of Algebra," "Problem Solving and Data Analysis," "Passport to Advanced Math," and "Additional Topics in Math." The no-calculator section will not contain any "Problem Solving and Data Analysis" questions. Each section of the test will contain *reference information* at the beginning that includes a number of geometric proportions and formulas, such as area formulas, the Pythagorean Theorem, special right triangles, and volume formulas.

If you want to zero in on the concepts you need to review, take a free practice test (at www.collegeboard.org, for example) and score it yourself to identify the concepts behind any questions you miss. That way, you will know what you personally need to target as you study, in order to improve your score.

How to break down a question

The pages that follow will provide detailed descriptions of various approaches to problems on the Math Test: Straight-Up Textbook, Working the Question, Working the Answers, and Working the Test. Here's a quick summary of each approach:

- *Straight-Up Textbook*: This approach requires applying math concepts "the old-fashioned way" by using the strategies and content you've learned in school. That's why it is helpful to review all the concepts that will be tested. If you want to brush up your skills in specific areas, check out the Math Concepts Reference chapter beginning on page 147. Knowing when Straight-Up Textbook is the quickest route to the correct answer is a skill in itself!

- *Working the Question*: This approach is useful on problems that discuss number relationships without using specifics. Often those problems will rely on answers "in terms of" a variable or percent. Some of the nastiest-looking Math Test problems are not as bad as they seem once you learn to replace fuzzy variables with real numbers. A detailed explanation of this strategy begins on the next page.

- *Working the Answers*: This approach will serve you well on questions looking for a specific value as well as on questions that have many steps or seem particularly confusing. Working the Answers is a strategic way of working backwards from the answer choices in a way that actually *saves* time. A detailed explanation of this strategy begins on page 119.

- *Working the Test*: This approach is often useful for data analysis and geometry questions. It can also be a lifeline when you're running out of time. Working the Test is a collection of common things to check for in charts, graphs, and figures that will help you to eliminate answer choices that don't make sense. More complex than typical "eyeballing," but still simple enough to use quickly and effectively, Working the Test will help you to power through difficult questions with lots of details. A detailed explanation of this strategy begins on page 123.

Working the Question

Often on the SAT, Math questions will seem more like puzzles than solvable problems. It can feel like the test makers haven't given you enough information or are trying to "trick" you. The latter can be true on occasion—the SAT is a tricky test!—but not the former. **You will always be given enough information to solve the question.**

That's reassuring, right? Everything you need to get to the correct answer is right there in your test booklet. It's just a matter of using the given information properly and in the right order. With that in mind, let's talk about making the questions work *for* you on Math sections. Consider this sample question:

> If n is a negative odd integer, then which of the following will be a positive even integer?
> (A) $4n$
> (B) $-6n$
> (C) $\frac{n}{2}$
> (D) $3n^2$

This type of question can be intimidating because it relies completely upon your knowledge of number properties and comfort level with variables. However, there is a quicker way to work through this question. It is a method that will both save you time on straightforward questions and help you to get through tougher questions.

Working the Question: When a question works in terms of variables or variable expressions (usually with variables in the answer choices), replace the variable with an easy-to-work-with number that suits the question. Solve the question in terms of that number. Once you have an answer, plug the number you chose into the variables in the answer choices. The correct answer choice will match your solution to the question.

Cecil's Tips to Stay Sharp

Yes, you could pick -347 for n in this question, but why would you? -3 is a perfectly usable number, and as long as you follow the constraints of the question, your number will lead to the right answer.

This means that, rather than working with the nebulous *n*, we will select a number that *could* be *n* and apply it to the answer choices to find the one that works. For example, let's say that *n* is equal to -3. That fits the question's requirements of being a "negative odd integer," and it is a small, simple number.

You might wonder why we didn't suggest choosing -1. In general, it is a good policy to **steer clear of choosing -1, 0, or 1 when Working the Question**, since those numbers have exceptional "behaviors" when they are multiplied, raised to powers greater than 1, and so on.

It's not that -1, 0, or 1 won't work—as long as they fit within the restrictions of the question, they will—but you will be more likely to have multiple answer choices work out, meaning you'll have to work through the question again with replacement numbers. Do yourself a favor by choosing other numbers from the start.

So now the question becomes, "If -3 is a negative odd integer, then which of the following will be a positive even integer?"

All you have to do now is replace *n* with -3 in each of the answer choices and see which one equals a positive even integer. That's it!

(A) $4n = 4 * -3 = -12$ *not positive*
(B) $-6n = -6 * -3 = 18$ **positive, even, and an integer!**
(C) $\frac{n}{2} = -\frac{3}{2}$ *not positive, not even, not an integer*
(D) $3n^2 = 3(-3 * -3) = 27$ *not even*

See how that made the answer clearer? Keep in mind that, when Working the Question, **you should check every answer for a match**, just in case you happened to pick a number that works for more than one answer. If that happens, simply pick another number, work through the problem again, and check both answers again. No big deal.

With a bit of practice, Working the Question saves you time, simplifies the questions, and makes the SAT Math Test a whole lot less wicked.

So let's practice this strategy! We'll start with a straightforward question.

Straightforward:

Sara can braid b bracelets in an hour. If she plans to give r bracelets to each of her three friends, then how many hours will Sara need to make all the bracelets?

(A) rb
(B) $br/3$
(C) $3r/b$
(D) $3rb$

This question involves both rates and variables, but we can eliminate the trickiest elements from the problem by Working the Question: replace b with an easy-to-work-with number, like 2. Replace r with an easy-to-work-with number as well; since you're working with rates, it's often helpful to choose numbers that divide evenly into one another. Let's say that r is 4.

Using those simple numbers, the question becomes one of quick arithmetic: "Sara can braid **2** bracelets in an hour. If she plans to give **4** bracelets to each of her three friends, then how many hours will Sara need to make all the bracelets?"

$$4 \; bracelets \; per \; friend * 3 \; friends = 12 \; bracelets$$

$$12 \; bracelets / 2 \; bracelets \; per \; hour = \mathbf{6 \; hours}$$

Now that we have an answer with numbers, just plug in 2 for n and 4 for p in the answer choices, and see which one equals 6.

(A) rb $2 * 4 = 8$
(B) $br/3$ $4 * 2 / 3 = 8/3$
(C) $3r/b$ $3 * 4 / 2 = 12/2 = \mathbf{6}$
(D) $3rb$ $3 * 4 * 2 = 24$

Using the question makes it clear that **C** is the correct answer—no zany-looking algebra, conversions, or formulas required. And remember, the bonus of using this strategy even on questions that you could solve algebraically is that, with practice, it will save you time on the SAT and give you more minutes to devote to those *eeeevil* questions at the end of the section.

Cecil's Tips to Stay Sharp

Since "percent" literally means "per hundred," always start by choosing 100 for percents questions, even if it means assuming that a tablet costs 100 dollars. You will save valuable time and steps by not needing to convert back from another number.

Let's move on to a more challenging question.

Complex:

Big Buy Electronics was selling tablets for *s* dollars each. During a store sale, the price of the tablets was reduced by *y* percent. One tablet did not sell and was further reduced by 15 percent for clearance. What was the final price of this tablet, in terms of *s* and *y*?

(A) $1.15(s - y)$
(B) $0.85s - 1.15y$
(C) $s - y - 15$
(D) $0.85s(1 - \frac{y}{100})$

Percents problems are ideal for Working the Question.

Assuming the tablet's original cost was 100 dollars ($s = 100$), let's choose a number for *y*. How about 25? It's a multiple of 5 and a factor of 100, which make it an easy-to-work-with choice in this percents question.

If $y = 25$, then the tablet's $100 original price was first dropped by 25%, or $25, to $75. See? No converting!

Next, the price was reduced by an additional 15%. *This does not mean* another 15 dollars! It means 15% of the lowered price.

15% of $75 is $11.25, leaving us with a final clearance price of $75 - $11.25 = ***$63.75***

Same as before—now that we have an answer for the numbers we substituted for *s* and *y*, plug those same numbers into the answer choices and see which one matches:

(A) $1.15s - y$ $1.15(100 - 25) = 1.15(75) = 86.25$
(B) $0.85s - 1.15y$ $.85 * 100 - 1.15 * 25 = 85 - 28.75 = 56.25$
(C) $s - y - 15$ $100 - 25 - 15 = 60$
(D) $.85s(1 - \frac{y}{100})$ $.85 * 100 (1 - .25) = 85(0.75) = \mathbf{63.75}$

No worries! Only answer **D** works, so you're done. Ready for an *eeeevil* question?

Eeeevil:

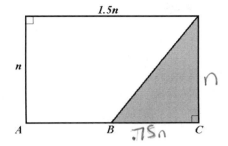

In the rectangle above, B is the midpoint of A and C. In terms of n, what is the perimeter of the shaded region?

(A) $3n$
(B) $.75n$
(C) $1.5n$
(D) n

This is a great example of a question that *could* be solved algebraically, but *should* be solved by Working the Question to save time. Also, if you are unsure of how to begin a problem like this, you can always start by choosing a number to replace the variable, since it occurs in the question and in the answer choices. It's all in terms of n, so if we just pick a number to substitute for n, then we will take a messy geometry-algebra hybrid back to its arithmetic roots… with a little help from the Pythagorean Theorem.

Since you're working with $1.5n$, it's a good idea to pick a number that's divisible by 2—suppose n equals 6. Knowing that AB equals BC in length (since B is the midpoint), let's fill in the diagram with some solid numbers.

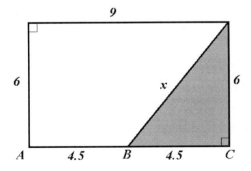

Yes, there is still a pesky variable—the unknown length of the shaded region. Fortunately, it is the hypotenuse of a right triangle, and we know the lengths of both the triangle's legs. Pythagorean Theorem time!

$$a^2 + b^2 = c^2$$

$$4.5^2 + 6^2 = x^2$$

$$20.25 + 36 = x^2$$

$$56.25 = x^2$$

$$7.5 = x$$

Now that we know the length of the unknown side, we can find the **perimeter** of the shaded region, which is what the question asked for.

$$4.5 + 6 + 7.5 = 18$$

Whatever number you picked to use for *n* in the question will also work for the correct answer choice. So, just plug **6**, our substitute for *n*, into the answer choices and see which comes out **18**:

(A)	$3n$	$3 * 6 =$ **18**
(B)	$.75n$	$.75 * 6 = 4.5$
(C)	$1.5n$	$1.5 * 6 = 9$
(D)	n	6

Perfect! When you use what the question gives you and substitute it into the answer choices, there's no messy wrangling with everything in terms of *x*—just a calm, methodical path through the answer choices to **A**, the correct answer. And it's a method that works no matter how difficult the question is.

Huzzah! You've conquered an *eeeevil* SAT Math question! You really can make the questions work for you on any Math problem that works in terms of variables. Check out the Math Practice Set chapter beginning on page 209 for more practice.

Cecil's Tips to Stay Sharp

Always make sure to double-check that you answer what the question is asking, especially on questions with many steps or varying units. It would be awful to miss a question that you otherwise solved perfectly because you stopped one step too soon!

Working the Answers

Hopefully you feel like the SAT Math problems that ask you to work in terms of fuzzy variables are a lot less vague now. And that's great! But what about problems like this?

> In a community soccer league, there are 7 more girls than boys. The league has 51 players overall. How many boys are in the league?
>
> (A) 18
> (B) 20
> (C) 22
> (D) 24

There are no variables in this question, so Working the Question won't help you here. But never fear! There's another strategy you can use on questions like these. It's basically the opposite of Working the Question—that's why it's called Working the Answers.

Working the Answers: When a question asks you "how many" or gives you number values in the answer choices (usually integers), <u>strategically</u> plug the answer choices back into the question to see if they check out.

This method is a systematic version of what people often do on standardized tests anyway: guess and check. The trouble with "guess and check" is that it's often done in times of panic, in a haphazard way. This wastes valuable time and stresses you out. Working the Answers puts you back in the driver's seat and actually *saves* time. Here's how:

1. The answer choices are arranged in ascending or descending order, so the first answer you plug into the question should be a middle answer (**B** or **C**). If it checks out, great! You're done! High-fives all around!

2. If it doesn't work out, consider whether the answer you tried first is too big or too small. If it is too big, you can eliminate it, along with any bigger answers. Likewise, if it is too small, then eliminate it and anything smaller. Then try the next-closest answer.

3. Either that answer will work, or you'll be able to eliminate it too, leaving only one answer that *must* be right. For those of you keeping score at home, this means you only need to try *two* answers max to get the correct one.

The only exception to this is when a question asks for the greatest or least possible number. If you are asked for the greatest possible number, start with answer choice **D** (the greatest answer choice) and work up through the answers until you find one that works.

Likewise, if you are asked for the least possible number, start with choice **A** (the least answer choice) and work your way down.

Working the Answers saves you time, minimizes the need for complicated algebraic expressions, and avoids that stressful guess-and-check feeling. So let's try it with that pesky soccer league question.

> In a community soccer league, there are 7 more girls than boys. The league has 51 players overall. How many boys are in the league?
>
> (A) 18
> (B) 20
> (C) 22
> (D) 24

Let's start by assuming **B** is the answer—say there are 20 boys in the league.

$$20 \text{ boys} + (20 + 7) \text{ girls} = 47 \text{ players}$$

We got 47 as the answer, but the question tells us that there are 51 players. **B** is too small! That means **A** is also too small, so we can eliminate both answers at once. Let's plug in answer **C** instead. Either it will work, or **D** will have to be the answer.

$$22 \text{ boys} + (22 + 7) \text{ girls} = 51 \text{ players}$$

Answer choice **C** gives us an answer that matches the question, so we know that it's correct and can move right along—after only trying two answers! Just keep your cool, and Working the Answers will save you time and make the SAT Math section a whole lot less *eeeevil*.

Now let's practice this strategy! We'll start with a straightforward question.

Straightforward:

> Tommy, Jackson, and Bennett have been collecting stamps. Jackson has three times as many stamps as Tommy, but only half as many as Bennett. If Bennett has 72 stamps, then how many does Tommy have?
>
> (A) 12
> (B) 15
> (C) 18
> (D) 24

Once again, let's start by assuming **B** is the answer—say that Tommy has 15 stamps. We're going to have to work from Tommy to Bennett to see if this number matches up.

$Tommy = 15$
$Jackson = 3 * Tommy = 45$
Jackson has half as many as Bennett, so:
$Bennett = 45 * 2 = 90$

Wait a sec, the question told us that Bennett only has 72 stamps. 90 is too many, which means that 15 is too many for Tommy to have.

Eliminate **B**, **C**, and **D**, leaving only **A** as the correct answer! We only had to try *one* answer to get to the right one. Think about how much time that would save you on the test!

All right, speed demon, ready for another?

Complex:

> Kiera is selling her ceramics at an art show. She sells mugs for $8 profit each and bowls for $6 profit each. If Kiera sold both types of items and made a profit of $112, what is the greatest number of mugs she could have sold?
> (A) 9
> (B) 11
> (C) 12
> (D) 14

$8m + 6b = 112$

In this case, we should start with answer choice **D**, because the question asks for the greatest possible number. Once an answer choice works, we'll be done!

But this complex question requires a little more critical reasoning. The $8 mug profits and $6 bowl profits need to add up to $112, and we know that at least one of each item was sold. That means the profit on mugs alone should be a multiple of 8, *and* whatever is left over must be a multiple of 6 to account for the bowls. Make sense?

Now let's try the answers, starting with **D**:

(D)   14 $mugs * \$8/mug = \$112$
This tricky answer looks right, but there's nothing left over to account for the bowls. Next!

(C)   12 $mugs * \$8/mug = \$96$
The amount left over is $16, which is not divisible by 6.
Onward!

(B)   11 $mugs * \$8/mug = \$88$
The leftover profit here is $24, which is divisible by 6!

We don't have to bother with answer **A** here, since the question asks for the greatest number that works, and 11 is greater than 9. **B** is the answer, and we can move on!

Ready for an *eeeevil* question?

Eeeevil:

An artisan at a basket factory is responsible for the following tasks: weaving a basket, trimming the edges, and attaching a binding. This artisan takes x minutes to attach a binding, $2x$ minutes to trim the edges, and $7x$ minutes to weave each basket. If the artisan can complete 19 baskets in an eight-hour shift, then how long does it take him, to the nearest minute, to trim the edges of one basket?
(A) 4
(B) 5
(C) 6
(D) 7

Whew, this is a nasty new SAT problem. We're dealing with rates, a variable, and many pieces of information that are all relative to each other. Don't panic! You will always be given enough information to solve the problem, so take a moment to organize it.

If the artisan takes x minutes to attach a binding, $2x$ minutes to trim the edges, and $7x$ minutes to weave a basket, then the time spent on one basket can be split up into 10 parts (that's $1 + 2 + 7$) of x minutes each. Another way of saying this is that it takes him $10x$ minutes to complete one basket. Sound good?

Now let's work the answers, starting with **B**; assume it takes him 5 minutes to trim one basket.

(B) $2x = 5$ minutes to trim one basket

   $x = 2.5$ minutes

   $10x$ minutes to complete a basket $= 25$ minutes per basket

   25 minutes $* 19$ baskets $= 475$ minutes

   $\dfrac{475 \text{ minutes}}{60 \text{ minutes per hour}} = 7.92$ hours

That's pretty darn close to eight hours—good enough to make **B** your answer for this question. If you were not pressed for time, you could try answer choice **C** to be sure:

(C) $6 = 2x$

   $x = 3$

   $10x$ mins per basket $= 30$ mins per basket

   30 minutes $* 19$ baskets $= 570$ minutes

   570 minutes $= 9.5$ hours

Yep, way too big, confirming that **B** is the right answer.

Bravo! You've conquered an *eeeevil* SAT Math question! You can make the answers work for you on most Math problems that ask you for values or "how many." Check out the Math Practice Set chapter beginning on page 209 for more practice.

Working the Test

With the strategies described in the previous sections (Working the Answers and Working the Question), you've got a couple of great tools for making it through confusing questions on the new SAT. And that's terrific! Hopefully you're also reviewing the foundational Math concepts discussed in this book as well, so that you will be ready to use your Straight-Up Textbook skills when necessary.

Cecil's Tips to Stay Sharp

You might think this problem would be more easily solved by starting at 8 hours and dividing down through the other units to solve for x. That's great and works just as well! The explanation on this problem is meant to illustrate how Working the Answers can be used on even the most complicated problems, so that you have an additional way to approach them.

However, there will be occasions on this standardized test when there will be a quicker path to the correct answer. You might even call it a ... well, a *shortcut*.

Now, hold up a second!

Before you think that this has morphed into your garden-variety test prep guide full of "tips and tricks," we want to remind you that the best thing you can do for your score on the SAT Math Test is to review the core content: the topics and methods that you have learned in algebra, geometry, and trigonometry classes at school.

The next best thing you can do is learn to apply strategies like Working the Question and Working the Answers, because they help you to bring complex-sounding problems back into your comfort zone.

After you've done those things, though, learning to Work the Test can help you with problems that would otherwise take a long time to solve. That help comes through picking out patterns, noticing key details, and applying a bit of logic here and there.

> ***Working the Test Strategy 1: When a question provides a graph or chart, you should check the scale and units, and then look for a pattern in the data.***

> ***Working the Test Strategy 2: If a question provides a drawn-to-scale geometric diagram, you can "eyeball" measurements and draw in additional information.***

> ***Working the Test Strategy 3: If a question is confusing or seems like it will take a lot of time, eliminate unrealistic answer choices to increase your odds of picking the right answer.***

Working the Test can save you time on problems that would otherwise be solved with complicated measurements or calculations. Let's try it out on a sample Math Test question.

> In the diagram below, the area of rectangle ABCD is 22 square inches. Point E is the midpoint of diagonal AC. What is the area of △AED in square inches?
> (A) 5.5
> (B) 6.5
> (C) 8
> (D) 11

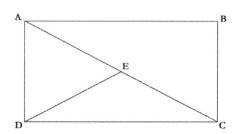

With a problem like this, your instinct might be to dive right into area formulas—that's totally fine! If you're comfortable solving a problem like this with Straight-Up Textbook math, then good for you. But what if there were a faster way, one that would leave you more time to devote to other questions?

That's where Working the Test comes in. Let's apply **Strategy 3** first: "Eliminate unreasonable answers." Since line segment AC is a diagonal, cutting the rectangle in half, triangle AED's area is definitely less than half of the total rectangle's area of 22. That means that **D** (11) is an unreasonable answer choice. Eliminate it! Even if you were pressed for time on this question and needed to guess, getting an unreasonable answer choice out of the way means that you're more likely to choose the right one.

Now let's apply **Strategy 2**: "Eyeball measurements and draw in additional information." You can trust this diagram since it doesn't have the "not drawn to scale" disclaimer. When you're eyeballing, don't hesitate to break up figures into smaller, more manageable shapes, like this:

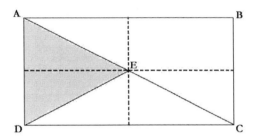

The problem divided the rectangle along diagonals, which can distort the way the sections look on the page. By adding dotted lines to break this rectangle in a more familiar way (smaller rectangles), we can see a clearer division.

The vertical dotted line cuts the rectangle in half, and the horizontal line makes it plain that half of the rectangle can be divided into four equal triangles. That means the whole rectangle is made up of *eight* equal triangles.

Triangle AED (shaded) contains two of the rectangle's eight equal triangles, so triangle AED's area must be equal to $\frac{2}{8}$ (or $\frac{1}{4}$) of the rectangle's total area of 22 units.

$$\frac{1}{4} * 22 = 5.5$$

How about that? One quick calculation and this puzzling problem is finished!

Now let's work through a few questions of varying difficulty, using the Working the Test strategies to save time and legwork on messy-looking problems.

Straightforward:

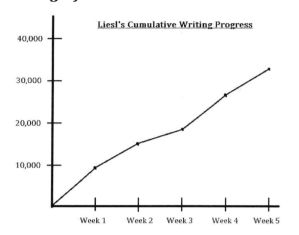

Week #	Words written per week
1	9,403
2	5,767
3	3,201
4	8,558
5	6,006

Liesl is writing a novel. To stay motivated she keeps a log of how many words she writes. Liesl's goal is to write 40,000 words of her novel within six weeks. The cumulative line graph and chart above show Liesl's progress through the first five weeks. How many words will she need to write per day (on average) during each of the remaining seven days to meet her goal by the end of the sixth week?

(A) 858
(B) 1,009
(C) 1,343
(D) 4,705

Don't let the different data representations throw you; they are basically presenting the same information. The line graph is cumulative, meaning that each week's sum of words is added to the previous week/s to keep a running total. The chart shows the number of words written during each week. Got it? And here's the great news about these two formats: *You only need one of them to get this question right.*

Work the Test here! Let's look at **Strategy 1** first: "Look for a pattern." Which data would you like to work with? Visual learners might prefer the line graph, because it gives a rough estimate of the total number of words completed by the end of Week 5: between 32,000 and 34,000 words. That means you can safely conclude that Liesl still needs to write somewhere around 7,000 words in the final week.

Remember what the question asks for: the average number of words per day. To get the average for Week 6, you should divide the weekly sum of words by the number of days. $\frac{7,000}{7} = 1,000$. That's almost spot-on with answer choice **B**! The other answer choices are different enough that you could stop here, choosing **B** as your answer.

If you're more of a numbers person, then go for a solid numbers approach. Add up the weekly totals given in the chart: 32,937. That means Liesl must write the 7,063 remaining words during Week 6. Divide that sum by 7 to get the daily average: 1,009. **B** it is!

And again, if charts and graphs just aren't your thing, or if you're running short on time, you can still increase your odds of getting the question right with Working the Test **Strategy 3**: "Eliminate unreasonable answers." Since the answer choices are averages for Week 6, you can multiply them each by 7 to see what sum they would give for the week:

(A) 858 * 7 = 6,006
(B) 1,009 * 7 = 7,063
(C) 1,343 * 7 = 9,401
(D) 4,705 * 7 = 32,935

Among those answer choices, **D** is unreasonably large and can be eliminated. If you check the space above the last point on the line graph before the 40,000 mark—definitely more than 5,000 but less than 10,000—you can tell that **B** is the safest choice as the number closest to the middle.

Terrific! Several paths to the right answer and none of them will take up much time. Are you ready to take it up a notch?

Complex:

David was driving from Harrisburg, Pennsylvania to Tarrytown, New York. He traveled at an average speed of 60 miles per hour for the first three hours of the trip. David then encountered a traffic jam, so for the last hour of the trip he averaged 20 miles per hour. What was David's average speed for the entire trip?

(A) 35 mph
(B) 40 mph
(C) 45 mph
(D) 50 mph

Averaging rates is tricky because they are **weighted** differently; that means that one rate counts for more than the other. (For more information on how weighted averages work, check out Concept #23 in the Math Concepts Reference chapter). In this problem, it means that David traveled at two different rates of speed, each for a different length of time. The average speed should *not* just split the difference. This is where you should apply Working the Test **Strategy 3**: "Eliminate unreasonable answers."

David traveled much longer at 60 miles per hour, so the average speed for the entire trip should be closer to 60 than it is to 20. That means that answers **A** and **B** are too small and can be immediately eliminated. You're already down to only two possible answers! If you were running out of time on a section, you would have much better odds of picking the right answer… and you might lean towards **D** as the closer answer to 60.

To be completely sure of your answer, though, you can quickly set up an average equation that takes the weighting out of the problem. To calculate average rate of speed (miles per hour), you need to *divide the total distance traveled by the total time*, like this:

$(60 \; mph * 3 \; hours) + (20 \; mph * 1 \; hour) = 180 + 20 = 200 \; miles \; total$

$$\frac{200 \; miles}{4 \; hours} = 50 \; miles \; per \; hour$$

And there you have it! A straightforward calculation confirms what you could deduce by Working the Test: **D** is the correct answer.

All right, now let's take this strategy to an *eeeevil* question.

Eeeevil:

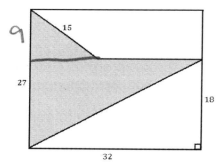

Tom is cutting a decorative shape for a poster out of a rectangular piece of cardstock that measures 32 centimeters by 27 centimeters, as shown above. The decorative shape, represented by the shaded region, will be covered in superfine glitter. How many square centimeters of cardstock will Tom cover in glitter?

(A) 98
(B) 288
(C) 342
(D) 576

This question sounds like a hot mess covered in glitter (which incidentally is probably what Tom will look like once he finishes the poster). However, two of the Working the Test strategies will help you get much closer to an answer choice very quickly.

First, there's **Strategy 2**: "Eyeball measurements and draw in additional information." The odd shape of the shaded region becomes much more familiar with the addition of one line to split it into two right triangles, like this:

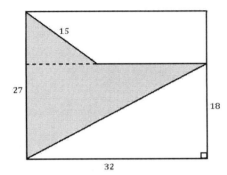

From this addition to the diagram, you can now make two additional conclusions that will help you employ **Strategy 3**: "Eliminate unreasonable answers."

The area of the shaded region is less than half of the whole diagram's area: 27 * 32, or 864 units.

The area of the shaded region is also greater than the area of the larger shaded triangle: $\frac{1}{2}(18)(32)$, or 288 units.

In other words, $288 <$ *shaded area* < 864. This again eliminates two answer choices from contention, leaving only **C** and **D**. You could additionally conclude that the area of the smaller shaded triangle is much less than 288, so answer **D** is much too big.

C for the win!

And here's how to be extra sure, in case you'd like to check your work:

1. Split the side length of 27, based on the side length of 18 across from it, into segments of 9 and 18 units.

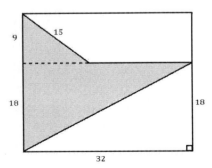

2. Use the Pythagorean Theorem to solve for the base (other leg) of the smaller shaded triangle. $9^2 + b^2 = 15^2$ → $49 + b^2 = 225$ → $b^2 = 144$ → $b = 12$

3. Use the base of 12 and height of 9 to solve for the area of the smaller triangle: $\frac{1}{2}(9)(12) = 54$

4. Add 54 to the other shaded triangle's area (288) to find the total shaded area: 342.

Excellent! You've conquered another *eeeevil* SAT Math question! You can Work the Test on many SAT Math questions to save time and help you feel more in control.

A Final Note

The strategies discussed in this chapter will not work on every single question on the Math Test. However, in addition to helping you work your way to the right answers on a great number of questions, with practice these strategies will save you a lot of time and brain power—time and brain power that you can devote to the remaining questions by using your Straight-Up Textbook skills.

Read on for mental math drills and concept reviews that will sharpen your old-fashioned math skills. Then as you practice, remember to Work the Questions, Work the Answers, Work the Test… In other words, make the SAT Math Test work for you!

Chapter 8: Calculator-Free Math Drills

As mentioned in the previous chapter, the new SAT Math Test includes a 25-problem section for which no calculators will be permitted. Whether you're a mental math enthusiast or a total calculator devotee, this chapter's calculator-free drills will help you to practice and boost your speed for the test. Here are the drills you'll find in this chapter in order of presentation:

- Addition
- Subtraction
- Multiplication
- Division
- Fractions and Decimals
- Factors and Multiples
- Exponents

We hope that you find these drills helpful in improving your mental math skills. Good luck!

Addition

Work through this page as quickly as you can. No calculator! (Answers on page 139.)

1. 15 + 31 =
2. 46 + 27 =
3. 8 + 16 =
4. 79 + 50 =
5. 61 + 17 =
6. 75 + 50 =
7. 125 + 175 =
8. 7 + 38 =
9. 112 + 63 =
10. 230 + 340 =
11. 136 + 77 =
12. 15 + 35 =
13. 48 + 62 =
14. 570 + 280 =
15. 128 + 128 =
16. 180 + 45 =
17. 13 + 37 =
18. 5400 + 630 =
19. 1325 + 1750 =
20. 691 + 153 =
21. 87 + 97 =
22. 70 + 180 =
23. 90 + 75 =
24. 360 + 720 =
25. 16.5 + 14.3 =
26. 0.97 + 0.17 =
27. 0.112 + 0.8 =
28. 1.4 + 2.65 =
29. 7.85 + 6.25 =
30. 0.987 + 0.123 =

Subtraction

Work through this page as quickly as you can. No calculator! (Answers on page 140.)

1. $17 - 9 =$

2. $24 - 18 =$

3. $50 - 25 =$

4. $56 - 17 =$

5. $28 - 11 =$

6. $90 - 65 =$

7. $100 - 36 =$

8. $227 - 141 =$

9. $350 - 125 =$

10. $433 - 56 =$

11. $360 - 120 =$

12. $54 - 18 =$

13. $60 - 15 =$

14. $87 - 93 =$

15. $-14 - 17 =$

16. $36 - 72 =$

17. $100 - 350 =$

18. $575 - 676 =$

19. $142 - 200 =$

20. $6500 - 3750 =$

21. $4862 - 53 =$

22. $26.5 - 18 =$

23. $4.35 - 2.17 =$

24. $6.1 - 0.9 =$

25. $19.4 - 20.6 =$

26. $1.5 - 7.5 =$

27. $3.21 - 1.28 =$

28. $0.999 - 1 =$

29. $5.65 - 2.3 =$

30. $5.25 - 3.75 =$

Multiplication

Work through this page as quickly as you can. No calculator! (Answers on page 141.)

1. $3 * 8 =$
2. $12 * 5 =$
3. $10 * 7 =$
4. $4 * 6 =$
5. $3 * 13 =$
6. $2 * 25 =$
7. $7 * 7 =$
8. $9 * 4 =$
9. $10 * 15 =$
10. $20 * 30 =$
11. $4 * 50 =$
12. $5 * 16 =$
13. $1.4 * 4 =$
14. $250 * 0.5 =$
15. $40 * 1.5 =$
16. $90 * 6 =$
17. $100 * 360 =$
18. $300 * 40 =$
19. $9 * 150 =$
20. $50 * 50 =$
21. $3.6 * 20 =$
22. $16 * 16 =$
23. $5 * 170 =$
24. $19 * 30 =$
25. $4.9 * 7 =$
26. $52 * 4 =$
27. $18 * 20 =$
28. $45 * 1.2 =$
29. $50 * 60 =$
30. $350 * 40 =$

Division

Work through this page as quickly as you can. Some problems may have a decimal or remainder. No calculator! (Answers on page 142.)

1. $\dfrac{35}{5} =$
2. $\dfrac{24}{6} =$
3. $\dfrac{39}{3} =$
4. $\dfrac{54}{9} =$
5. $\dfrac{12}{4} =$
6. $\dfrac{26}{2} =$
7. $\dfrac{50}{5} =$
8. $\dfrac{60}{12} =$
9. $\dfrac{100}{5} =$
10. $\dfrac{75}{25} =$
11. $\dfrac{160}{8} =$
12. $\dfrac{200}{4} =$
13. $\dfrac{150}{10} =$
14. $\dfrac{500}{25} =$
15. $\dfrac{360}{90} =$

16. $\dfrac{120}{2} =$
17. $\dfrac{100}{8} =$
18. $\dfrac{3.6}{3} =$
19. $\dfrac{24}{1.5} =$
20. $\dfrac{720}{60} =$
21. $\dfrac{300}{2.5} =$
22. $\dfrac{81}{4} =$
23. $\dfrac{0.8}{0.5} =$
24. $\dfrac{240}{8} =$
25. $\dfrac{810}{90} =$
26. $\dfrac{200}{3} =$
27. $\dfrac{650}{13} =$
28. $\dfrac{2000}{2.5} =$
29. $\dfrac{1000}{\frac{1}{4}} =$
30. $\dfrac{4900}{70} =$

Fractions and Decimals

Convert the following fractions into decimals. No calculator! (Answers on page 143.)

1. $\frac{3}{4} =$

2. $\frac{7}{2} =$

3. $\frac{4}{5} =$

4. $\frac{5}{4} =$

5. $\frac{9}{10} =$

6. $\frac{25}{10} =$

7. $\frac{9}{6} =$

8. $\frac{2}{3} =$

9. $\frac{4}{9} =$

10. $\frac{7}{8} =$

11. $\frac{48}{5} =$

12. $\frac{60}{8} =$

13. $\frac{25}{4} =$

14. $\frac{5}{9} =$

15. $\frac{56}{3} =$

16. $\frac{125}{200} =$

Convert the following decimals into fractions in lowest terms. No calculator! (Answers on page 143.)

17. $0.25 =$

18. $4.6 =$

19. $5.5 =$

20. $0.34 =$

21. $0.88 =$

22. $0.7 =$

23. $3.6\overline{6} =$

24. $2.25 =$

25. $11.3\overline{3} =$

26. $9.75 =$

27. $2.4 =$

28. $4.5\overline{5} =$

29. $1.2 =$

30. $3.5 =$

Multiples and Factors

List the first eight multiples of each of the following numbers. No calculator! (Answers on page 144.)

1. 4
2. 7
3. 3
4. 11
5. 6

6. 15
7. 8
8. 20
9. 13
10. 25

List all the factors of each of the following numbers. No calculator! (Answers on page 144.)

11. 40
12. 54
13. 36
14. 75
15. 64

16. 88
17. 130
18. 200
19. 168
20. 360

Exponents

Simplify the following exponents as quickly as you can. No calculator! (Answers on page 145.)

1. 5^2

2. 4^3

3. 6^2

4. 7^2

5. 3^3

6. 2^5

7. 10^3

8. 12^2

9. $\left(\frac{1}{6}\right)^3$

10. $\left(\frac{1}{4}\right)^4$

11. 10^{-2}

12. $\left(\frac{1}{2}\right)^2$

13. $\left(-\frac{3}{4}\right)^3$

14. $\left(\frac{1}{4}\right)^{-2}$

15. $\left(\frac{1}{3}\right)^3$

16. 5^{-3}

17. $36^{-\frac{1}{2}}$

18. $8^{\frac{2}{3}}$

19. $(2^3)^2$

20. $169^{\frac{1}{2}}$

21. $\left(\frac{3}{4}\right)^{-2}$

22. $(4^{-2})^2$

23. 15^2

24. $(-30)^2$

25. $(10^3)^2$

26. 5^4

27. $3^2 * 3^2$

28. $4^2 * 2^3$

Addition Drill Answers

1.	46		16.	225
2.	73		17.	50
3.	24		18.	6,030
4.	129		19.	3,075
5.	78		20.	844
6.	125		21.	184
7.	300		22.	250
8.	45		23.	165
9.	175		24.	1,080
10.	570		25.	30.8
11.	213		26.	1.14
12.	50		27.	0.912
13.	110		28.	4.05
14.	850		29.	14.1
15.	256		30.	1.11

Subtraction Drill Answers

1.	8	16.	-36
2.	6	17.	-250
3.	25	18.	-101
4.	39	19.	-58
5.	17	20.	2,750
6.	25	21.	9
7.	64	22.	8.5
8.	86	23.	2.18
9.	225	24.	5.2
10.	377	25.	-1.2
11.	240	26.	-6
12.	36	27.	1.93
13.	45	28.	-0.001
14.	-6	29.	3.35
15.	-31	30.	1.8

Multiplication Drill Answers

1. 24
2. 60
3. 70
4. 24
5. 39
6. 50
7. 49
8. 36
9. 150
10. 600
11. 200
12. 80
13. 5.6
14. 125
15. 60
16. 540
17. 36,000
18. 12,000
19. 1,350
20. 2,500
21. 72
22. 256
23. 850
24. 570
25. 34.3
26. 208
27. 360
28. 54
29. 3,000
30. 14,000

Division Drill Answers

1.	7	16.	60
2.	4	17.	12.5
3.	13	18.	1.2
4.	6	19.	16
5.	3	20.	12
6.	13	21.	120
7.	10	22.	20.25
8.	5	23.	1.6
9.	20	24.	30
10.	3	25.	9
11.	20	26.	$66.\overline{6}$
12.	50	27.	50
13.	15	28.	800
14.	20	29.	4,000
15.	4	30.	70

Fractions and Decimals Drill Answers

Fractions:

1. 0.75
2. 3.5
3. 0.8
4. 1.25
5. 0.9
6. 2.5
7. 1.5
8. $0.\overline{6}$
9. $0.\overline{4}$
10. 0.875
11. 9.6
12. 7.5
13. 6.25
14. $0.\overline{5}$
15. $18.\overline{6}$
16. 0.625

Decimals:

17. $\frac{1}{4}$
18. $\frac{23}{5}$
19. $\frac{11}{2}$
20. $\frac{17}{50}$
21. $\frac{22}{25}$
22. $\frac{7}{10}$
23. $\frac{11}{3}$
24. $\frac{9}{4}$
25. $\frac{34}{3}$
26. $\frac{39}{4}$
27. $\frac{12}{5}$
28. $\frac{41}{9}$
29. $\frac{6}{5}$
30. $\frac{7}{2}$

Multiples and Factors Drill Answers

Multiples:

1. 4, 8, 12, 16, 20, 24, 28, 32
2. 7, 14, 21, 28, 35, 42, 49, 56
3. 3, 6, 9, 12, 15, 18, 21, 24
4. 11, 22, 33, 44, 55, 66, 77, 88
5. 6, 12, 18, 24, 30, 36, 42, 48
6. 15, 30, 45, 60, 75, 90, 105, 120
7. 8, 16, 24, 32, 40, 48, 56, 64
8. 20, 40, 60, 80, 100, 120, 140, 160
9. 13, 26, 39, 52, 65, 78, 91, 104
10. 25, 50, 75, 100, 125, 150, 175, 200

Factors:

11. 1, 2, 4, 5, 8, 10, 20, 40
12. 1, 2, 3, 6, 9, 18, 27, 54
13. 1, 2, 3, 4, 6, 9, 12, 18, 36
14. 1, 3, 5, 15, 25, 75
15. 1, 2, 4, 8, 16, 32, 64
16. 1, 2, 4, 8, 11, 22, 44, 88
17. 1, 2, 5, 10, 13, 26, 65, 130
18. 1, 2, 4, 5, 8, 10, 20, 25, 40, 50, 100, 200
19. 1, 2, 3, 4, 6, 8, 12, 14, 21, 28, 42, 56, 84, 168
20. 1, 2, 3, 4, 5, 6, 8, 9, 10, 12, 15, 18, 20, 24, 30, 36, 40, 45, 60, 72, 90, 120, 180, 360

Exponents Drill Answers

1. 25
2. 64
3. 36
4. 49
5. 27
6. 32
7. 1,000
8. 144
9. $\frac{1}{216}$
10. $\frac{1}{256}$
11. $\frac{1}{100}$
12. $\frac{1}{4}$
13. $-\frac{27}{64}$
14. 16
15. $\frac{1}{27}$
16. $\frac{1}{125}$
17. $\frac{1}{6}$
18. 4
19. 64
20. 13
21. $\frac{16}{9}$
22. $\frac{1}{256}$
23. 225
24. 900
25. 1,000,000
26. 625
27. 81
28. 128

Chapter 9: Math Concepts Reference

The 50 SAT Math concepts discussed in this chapter are intended to identify and explain the concepts you'll need to understand for the Math Test. If you're looking for a particular topic to review, refer to the index at the back of this book or to the list below.

Remember, each section of the Math Test will give **reference information** at the beginning that includes a number of geometric proportions and formulas. If a concept is in that group, it will be noted with the words, "***Included in Reference Information***."

For the new SAT the College Board (maker of the SAT) has delineated the overall concept areas of the Math Test with the following terms: "Heart of Algebra," "Problem Solving and Data Analysis," "Passport to Advanced Math," and "Other Topics in Math." Though we appreciate the originality of those titles, we have listed our concept areas a little differently here, just to make it a little clearer what's included in each.

- Arithmetic and Algebra: Concepts 1-19

- Statistics and Data Interpretation: Concepts 20-25

- Advanced Algebra: Concepts 26-33

- Geometry and Trigonometry: Concepts 34-47

- Miscellaneous Advanced Topics: Concepts 48-50

1. Apply the order of operations

Remember the order of algebraic operations with the acronym **PEMDAS**, or the mnemonic phrase "Please Excuse My Dear Aunt Sally." This order tells you how to perform algebraic operations when simplifying an expression or equation:

Parentheses	*Terms in parentheses need to be dealt with first—work from the inside out!*
Exponents	*Next, apply exponents (or powers) to any terms that have them.*
Multiplication/ Division	*These terms are equal in importance—just work from left to right.*
Addition/ Subtraction	*Again, these terms are equivalent—solve them from left to right.*

2. Simplify a one-variable expression

Simplifying a one-variable expression typically requires one or more of these steps: **combining like terms**, **distributing**, and **factoring**. Here's an example of simplifying an expression:

$5n + 3(n - 2)$	*Distribute the 3 (multiply both the n and the -2 by 3)*
$5n + 3n - 6$	*Combine like terms (add 5n and 3n)*
$8n - 6$	*The expression is now in its simplest state.*

3. Solve a one-variable equation or inequality

To solve a one-variable equation, you need to *isolate the variable*, which means to get it by itself on one side of the equation. This can be done by performing operations on both sides of the equation so that terms get combined or cancelled out, like this:

$3x + 5 = 4x - 1$ *Subtract 3x from both sides*

$5 = x - 1$ *Add 1 to both sides*

$6 = x$ *Now that x is **isolated**, we can see that it equals 6. No problem!*

Solving one-variable inequalities works the same way, except that you need to remember one additional rule: if you multiply or divide by a negative, you need to **reverse the sign**, like this:

$4n < 9n + 10$ *Subtract 9n from both sides*

$-5n < 10$ *Divide both sides by -5 **and** reverse the sign*

$n > -2$ *Now n is isolated, so we know that it must be greater than -2. Done!*

4. Multiply rational expressions

A rational expression is an expression (with or without a variable) that can be represented by a ratio or fraction. When you multiply rational expressions, simply multiply the numerators together and the denominators together, then reduce the fraction by dividing out common terms. For instance:

$\frac{4g}{5} * \frac{6}{2g}$ *Multiply the numerators to get 24g and the denominators to get 10g.*

$\frac{24g}{10g}$ *Divide out common terms (2 and g) to reduce the fraction.*

$\frac{12}{5}$ *The fraction cannot be reduced any further.*

5. Divide rational expressions

Dividing rational expressions is more straightforward than you might think. Reverse the numerator and denominator of the second rational expression to get its *reciprocal*, and then treat it as a multiplication, like this:

$\dfrac{\frac{42}{9}}{\frac{1}{3}}$ *Flip the second term (1/3) upside-down.*

$\dfrac{42}{9} * \dfrac{3}{1}$ *Now multiply instead...*

$\dfrac{126}{9}$ *... And simplify by dividing out 9.*

14 *That's it!*

6. Cross-multiply ratios

Cross-multiplication is a quick method for solving equations that contain ratios on both sides. Multiply the numerator on the left side of the equation by the denominator on the right, and multiply the numerator on the right by the denominator on the left. This saves the time you would spend multiplying and dividing terms individually. For instance:

$\dfrac{3x}{14} = \dfrac{12}{7}$ *Multiply 3x by 7 and 12 by 14.*

$21x = 168$ *Now divide both sides by 21 to isolate (solve for) x.*

$x = 8$ *Done!*

Keep in mind that you can only cross-multiply using the numerator of one side and the denominator of the other—it would not work to multiply both numerators or both denominators.

7. Solve for one variable in terms of another

Solving for one variable in terms of another means that you are just isolating one of them. SAT questions containing complicated word problems and multiple variables are often asking you to do this. Here's how to solve for one variable:

$3w + 4y = 24$ *Solve for w in terms of y (in other words, isolate w). Start by subtracting 4y from both sides.*

$3w = 24 - 4y$ *Then divide both sides by 3.*

$w = 8 - \frac{4}{3}y$ *Now w is by itself, so the expression on the other side of the equation is "in terms of y."*

8. Evaluate linear functions: domain, range, and graphing

A function works like a machine: **inputs**, also called *x*-values, are plugged into the function, the order of operations is followed, and the resulting numbers are the **outputs**, or *y*-values. A function is written as an equation with two variables, usually expressed as *x* and *y*, or *x* and *f(x)*.

In order to be a function, the equation must have no more than one output for each input. That makes sense, right? A machine wouldn't work if you had more than one possible outcome for an input—it wouldn't be reliable.

Functions can be graphed on the coordinate plane as lines, parabolas, and other shapes. Here is an example of a linear function, written out and then graphed:

$f(x) = \frac{1}{3}x + 2$

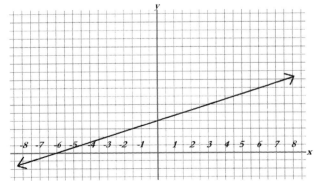

*The coefficients (number values) in this function indicate a **slope** of $\frac{1}{3}$ and a **y-intercept** of 2. Those indicate that the line crosses the y-axis at the point (0, 2) and that the line slants upward 1 unit for every 3 units it moves to the right.*

The possible *x*-values for a function are also known as the function's **domain**. Linear functions include all real numbers in their domains, because lines extend infinitely.

The possible *y*-values for a function are also known as the function's **range**. Linear functions *can* include all real numbers in their ranges, but if a linear function has a zero-value slope (for example, g*(x)* = 4), then it will graph as a flat line, and the range will be limited to the value listed in the function (i.e., 4).

9. Write a linear function in standard notation (slope-intercept)

The standard notation for a linear function is called **slope-intercept** form. This is a useful way to write the function because it clearly shows both the slope of the line and the y-intercept (where the line crosses the vertical axis). You might also have heard of this as *y* = ***mx*** + ***b*** format, where *m* represents slope and *b* represents the intercept. Here are some examples:

$f(x) = -2x + 5$ — *This line has a slope of -2 and crosses the y-axis at the point (0, 5).*

$g(x) = x + \frac{3}{2}$ — *This line has a slope of 1 and a y-intercept of 3/2.*

$h(x) = \frac{4}{5}x$ — *This line has a slope of 4/5. No number is given as the intercept, which means that this line crosses the y-axis at the point (0, 0).*

If a function is not given in standard notation—for example, 2*y* – 4*x* = 8—don't panic! Just solve for *y* in terms of *x*, and then you will have the function in standard notation.

10. Analyze a linear function graph

When you are given a linear function in standard notation, you can use the slope and intercept to graph it. You can also do the same thing in reverse, using the function's graph to observe its slope and intercept.

To calculate the slope, choose two points on the function's graph where you can clearly see the coordinate values—for instance, on the graph below, (-1,0) and (1,4). Remember, slope is "***rise over run***," which means the change in y-values over the change in x-values.

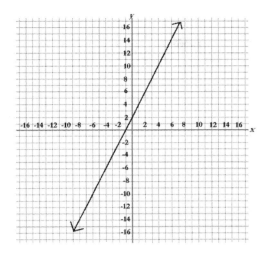

It's necessary that you keep the coordinate pairs in order, so if you're using $y_1 - y_2$ in the numerator, make sure to use $x_1 - x_2$ in the denominator, like this:

$\frac{4-0}{1-(-1)}$ *Use the positive coordinate pair first to make the subtraction easier.*

$\frac{4}{1+1} = \frac{4}{2} = 2$ *The ratio simplifies to 2, so that is the slope of this linear function.*

To evaluate the *y-intercept*, just look at the point where the line crosses the y-axis (vertical axis). This line crosses at the point (0,2), so 2 is the y-intercept. The standard notation, or slope-intercept form, of this function, is:

$f(x) = mx + b$ *Remember, m represents slope, and b represents y-intercept.*

$f(x) = 2x + 2$ *That's it!*

11. Work with divisibility: factors, multiples, and primes

Factors, multiples, and primes are best discussed together, because they are all matters of divisibility. Here are some key definitions and facts about these terms:

Factor: a whole number that can be evenly divided out of another number. For example, 3 is a factor of 6. 1 is a factor of every number.

Multiple: a whole number that is divisible by another number. For instance, 8 is a multiple of 4. Because 8 is a multiple of 4, any other multiple of 8 (16, 64, 2400…) will also be a multiple of 4. Every number is both a factor and a multiple of itself.

Prime number: a number that has only two factors: itself and 1. Primes cannot be negative because negative numbers are divisible by -1, and 1 is not prime because it only has one factor. Therefore, 2 is the smallest and the only even prime number. The first twelve prime numbers are: 2, 3, 5, 7, 11, 13, 17, 19, 23, 29, 31, 37.

Knowing how to efficiently find the factors and prime factors of a number is a very useful skill. Here are two methods to do just that: the T-chart and the factor tree.

A *T-chart* can be used to quickly generate all the factors of any number. Start by drawing a large uppercase T on scratch paper, and put the number in question on top; let's try 48.

The T creates two columns, which you will use to list the factors in pairs. Begin by putting 1 in the left column and 48 in the right, because every number has 1 and itself as factors.

Now go through 48's potential factors in ascending order.

Is 48 divisible by 2? Yes—so write 2 in the left column and 24 in the right.

Is 48 divisible by 3? Yes—and 16.

Is 48 divisible by 4? Yes—and 12.

Is 48 divisible by 5? No—so skip it.

Is 48 divisible by 6? Yes—and 8.

Is 48 divisible by 7? No—skip.

The next potential factor is 8, but we already have 8 in the right column. When a factor "crosses over" from left to right, that is the sign that you have included them all. And you're done!

Another quick way to factor a number—particularly if you want to take it down to prime factors—is to make a *factor tree*. Here's a factor tree of 48:

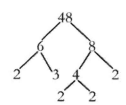

By beginning with the number in question and dividing all the way down until you get to primes, you can very quickly get the *prime factorization* of a number: 2 * 3 * 2 * 2 * 2 = 48.

This works no matter how you divide 48 at first—just keep dividing, and the tree will always take you down to the same prime numbers.

Greatest common factor (GCF)

The greatest common factor (GCF) is exactly what it sounds like: the greatest factor that certain numbers have in common. To find a GCF, you can use T-charts or factor trees. For the former, draw a T-chart for each number and identify the largest number that appears in both charts. For the latter, make a factor tree for each number, circle all the prime factors they have in common, and multiply all the circled factors of one tree together.

Here's an example—finding the greatest common factor of 105 and 189.

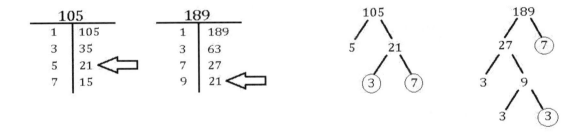

Greatest Common Factor = 3 * 7 = 21

Using either method, the GCF of 105 and 189—21—can quickly be found.

Least common multiple (LCM)

The least common multiple (LCM) is also just what it sounds like: the least multiple that specific numbers have in common. To find a LCM, consider whether the numbers in question have any factors in common. If not (e.g., 5 and 7), then multiplying them together will give you the LCM (35). If they do have factors in common, it gets a little more complex, like this:

What is the least common multiple of 4, 7, and 8?

You could just multiply 4, 7, and 8 together to get a common multiple (224), but how would you know if it's the *least* common multiple?

(Spoiler alert: it's not.)

Check the numbers. 7 is prime, but 4 and 8 have factors in common—namely, 2 and 4. As mentioned in the definition of "multiple" above, 8 is a multiple of 4, so any multiple of 8 will also be a multiple of 4. That means that you don't have to include that 4 at all!

With that pesky extra 4 out of the way, multiplying 7 and 8, which have no factors in common with each other, will give you the *least* common multiple: 56.

12. Solve a system of linear equations (substitution, combination)

When you are given a system of linear equations (meaning two or more) and asked to solve for the variables, you have several equally valid routes to a right answer. Let's work through these different methods using the following system of equations:

$$\begin{cases} 3x - y = 7 \\ 2x + 3y = 23 \end{cases}$$

The first is a tried-and-true method called **substitution**, and it works by solving for one variable at a time. First, you solve for one variable in terms of the other—remember, that means you isolate it (get it by itself). Let's work with the first equation first here, since y doesn't have a coefficient and will be easier to solve.

$3x - y = 7$ *Here's the equation. To get **y** by itself, subtract **3x** from both sides.*

$-y = -3x + 7$ *Now **y** is by itself, but it's negative. Multiply both sides by -1.*

$y = 3x - 7$ *With **y** by itself, we have solved for **y** in terms of **x**.*

Now comes the substitution part. Write out the second equation, but instead of y, write $(3x - 7)$. Then you'll have an equation that only has one variable—x—so you'll be able to solve for it.

$2x + 3y = 23$ *Here's the original equation. Replace **y** with (3x – 7).*

$2x + 3(3x - 7) = 23$

$2x + 9x - 21 = 23$ *Follow the order of operations to simplify terms and solve.*

$11x - 21 = 23$

$11x = 44$

$x = 4$ *Nailed it!*

You have an answer for *x*. Now go back to the first equation and plug it in to solve for *y*.

$3(4) - y = 7$

$12 - y = 7$

$-y = -5$

$y = 5$

There you go. Problem solved, with the aid of your friendly neighborhood substitution!

That might have seemed like a lot of steps to get to the right answer. Substitution is a dependable method that takes a little more legwork, but will always get you there. If you are more confident with mental math and want to move through a problem like this a little faster, you might prefer **combination** (also called **elimination**), which lets you knock out a variable more quickly. Let's try combination with the same system:

$$\begin{cases} 3x - y = 7 \\ 2x + 3y = 23 \end{cases}$$

With combination, you basically *add* the equations together. Look at the coefficients of the variables in the equations. The goal is to make one variable "cancel out" by having equal but opposite coefficients. Here, we have **3x** and **2x** (no easy matchup there) and **–y** and **3y**. If only it were **–3y** in that first equation…

But it can be!

If we multiply both sides of the first equation by –3, then our system would look like this:

$$\begin{cases} 9x - 3y = 21 \\ 2x + 3y = 23 \end{cases}$$

$11x + 0 = 44$

See? *y* is gone, leaving us with $11x = 44$. That's a quick solve to get $x = 4$, and then you can plug it into either equation to solve for *y*. If you see a way to eliminate a variable with this method, then **combination** can be a great time-efficient way to the answer.

There's still another way to work through a system of equations like this, believe it or not! It's good to know the first two ways for the no-calculator section, but the third way—the **calculator** way—is quick and painless. Remember our example system of equations?

$$\begin{cases} 3x - y = 7 \\ 2x + 3y = 23 \end{cases}$$

These two-variable equations are basically linear functions, and when you solve for *x* and *y*, you're actually solving for the coordinates of where these two functions intersect on the plane. Neat, right? So the way to use your graphing calculator (such as a TI-84 or TI-84 Plus) and solve them is pretty straightforward:

1. Solve for *y* in both equations so you have the functions in **slope-intercept form**.
2. Type both equations into your graphing calculator and view the graph.
3. Adjust the window and scale of your graph as needed.
4. Press the "CALC" button and select "Intersect."
5. Follow the prompts to select points on each graph and press "Enter."

Bingo! If you follow these steps, your calculator should spit out "$x = 4, y = 5$."

Technology can be so helpful—but it's also good to know the "old-fashioned" methods in case you need them. With **substitution**, **combination**, and **calculator** methods at your disposal, you'll be able to handle any systems the new SAT can throw at you!

13. Evaluate and convert between rates

A rate is any something-per-something: miles per gallon, dollars per pound, kilometers per hour, aliens per spaceship, etc. You can use a rate to start with one amount and solve for another amount. For instance:

> *Polly's Party Supply Store makes balloon bouquets using six inflated helium balloons and one weight for each balloon bouquet. If the store has 21 balloon weights in stock for a holiday, then how many balloons should Polly inflate to make as many bouquets as possible?*

The rate in this question is $6\frac{balloons}{bouquet}$, and you must work from the number of bouquets to the number of balloons. Setting up a ***proportion***—two rates equal to each other—is a speedy way to work through this question, because you can clearly match up the units.

$$\frac{6\ balloons}{1\ bouquet} = \frac{x\ balloons}{21\ bouquets}$$

*If there are 21 weights, Polly can make 21 bouquets. You can either note that **x** balloons should be 21 times as large as 6 balloons (because she's making 21 bouquets) or **cross-multiply** like the next step shown here.*

$$6\ balloons * 21\ bouquets = x\ balloons * 1\ bouquet$$

Cross-multiplying means multiplying the numerator (top number) of each side by the denominator (bottom number) of the other side. You'll know you did it right if you have one of each unit on each side.

$126 = x$ *Multiply and solve for x: 126 balloons.*

Cecil's Tips to Stay Sharp

Showing your work is helpful throughout the SAT Math Test, but especially when you're working with rates. Always note the units (abbreviated however you want) to make sure that you're keeping them straight!

The SAT Math Test can make rate questions more difficult by requiring you to convert from one rate to another. Each rate will always have two units, and the most important thing for you to do is *keep those units straight*. For example, you might see a question like this:

Jeremy is planning a weekend road trip of 180 miles in his new car, which averages 30 miles per gallon of gasoline. If gasoline costs $2.39 per gallon, then how much should Jeremy budget for gasoline for his trip, rounded up to the nearest dollar?

(A) *$12.00*
(B) *$15.00*
(C) *$18.00*
(D) *$20.00*

There are two different rates happening here—miles per gallon and dollars per gallon—and the question wants you to use the number of miles to determine the number of dollars. Let's solve it out, making sure to keep the rates straight by noting the units as we go.

$\frac{(180\ miles)}{\left(30 \frac{miles}{gallon}\right)} = 6\ gallons$ *The number of gallons is **constant**; now we can calculate dollars.*

$6\ gal * \frac{\$2.39}{(1\ gal)} = \$14.34$ *Rounding up gives an answer of $15.00, or **(B)**.*

See how keeping track of units makes this problem more straightforward? When multiplying or dividing by rates, you can cancel out units accordingly (miles in the first step and gallons in the second) to make sure you're solving for the right thing.

Watch out for sneaky unit conversions on the SAT. If a question gives its details in terms of minutes but asks for an answer in terms of hours, you'll need to remember to convert those minutes to hours before marking your answer sheet. It can be helpful to convert to the final unit of measurement right away, or to circle the final unit to help you remember to do it later.

14. Use and calculate percents

Percents (often expressed as %) are a way of looking at a part of a whole, just like fractions or decimals. ***Percent*** literally means "per hundred," so using a percent effectively breaks up a number into 100 equal parts. For instance, if a question asked you, "44 equals what percent of 80?" you could set it up like this:

$\frac{44}{80} * 100 = 55\%$ *This means you're looking at 44 as a part of 80 and multiplying it by 100% (the 100 equal parts). 44 divided by 80 equals 0.55; when you multiply it by 100, you get 55. That means that 44 is 55% of 80.*

You could also look at it this way:

$44 = n * \frac{80}{100}$ *In this case you're dividing up 80 into 100 equal parts. Those 100 parts times **n** percent will equal 44. When you solve for **n**, it will still equal 55%.*

Some students prefer to work with one method over the other. Some like to punch in "44 / 80" on their calculators, get "0.55," and carry over two decimal points to convert to a percent. Whichever method works for you is perfectly fine! Just make sure that in any situation, you are using the *part* and the *whole* consistently.

15. Calculate percent change

It's important to recognize that percents are used in a number of ways on standardized tests. All that variety can make them trickier to work with. The first thing you will need to do is to assess what kind of percent you're dealing with in a question.

"25% *of* 200" means 25 of the 100 equal parts of 200.

$\quad$ This can be written as $\frac{25}{100} * 200$, which equals 50.

"25% *less/fewer than* 200" means 200 minus 25 of those 100 equal parts.

$\quad$ This can be written as $200 - (\frac{25}{100} * 200)$, which equals 150.

"25% *more/greater than* 200" means 200 plus 25 of those 100 equal parts.

$\quad$ This can be written as $200 + (\frac{25}{100} * 200)$, which equals 250.

A percent change, such as "The percent increase from 80 to 112" can be calculated in two ways. First, you can look at the difference between 112 (the *part*) and 80 (the *whole*) and multiply it by 100 percent, like this:

$\frac{112-80}{80} * 100 = \frac{32}{80} * 100 = 0.4 * 100 = 40\%$

Or you can find 112 as a percent *of* 80 and then subtract 100 percent from it, like this:

$\left(\frac{112}{80} * 100\right) - 100 = (1.4 * 100) - 100 = 140 - 100 = 40\%$

Again, either method is valid. Just figure out which one you like better and stick with it.

Watch out for problems in which percents change more than once, like this:

> *A furniture dealer purchased a couch at 20% less than its sticker price of $1000. He then marked up the couch by 40% from what he paid and sold it to a customer. What was the net (overall) percent increase from the sticker price to what the customer paid?*

You can bet that "20%" would be an answer choice here—it looks like the price dropped 20%, then increased 40%, so 20% would make sense…

But *don't be fooled!*

There are two percent changes here, and when you calculate the second one, you need to keep in mind that what you're taking a percent of is *different* than the first time. Look at it this way:

$1000 - \left(\frac{20}{100} * 1000\right) = 800$ *The 20% discount means that the dealer paid $800.*

$800 + \left(\frac{40}{100} * 800\right) = 1120$ *Now we add the markup: 40% of 800. That markup equals $320, so the customer paid $1120.*

With the new price calculated, we can figure out the percent increase from the sticker price ($1000) to the customer's price ($1120). First, 1120 is what percent *of* 1000?

$\frac{1120}{1000} * 100 = 112\%$ *The customer's price is 112% of the original price, so it is 12% greater than the original price.*

The net percent increase is 12%.

16. Convert among percents, decimals, and fractions

Just like you can say "exultant," "cheery," or "jovial" instead of "happy," you can use a decimal, percent, or fraction to describe an amount or ratio. They are different ways of expressing the same thing. Here are quick ways to convert among them:

From a decimal to a percent
>Multiply the decimal by 100 or move the decimal point two places to the right.
>>*Example: the decimal 1.43 converts to 143%*

From a decimal to a fraction
>If you don't recognize the equivalent fraction, then multiply the decimal by 100 and set it as a fraction over 100. Then reduce the fraction by dividing out common factors until the fraction is in its lowest terms.
>>*Example: 0.75 becomes $\frac{75}{100}$. Now reduce the fraction: $\frac{75}{100} = \frac{15}{20} = \frac{3}{4}$*

From a percent to a decimal
>Divide the percent by 100 or move the decimal point two places to the left.
>>*Example: the percent 20% converts to 0.2*

From a percent to a fraction
>Since percent means "per hundred," just set the percent as a fraction over 100 and then reduce it to lowest terms.
>>*Example: the percent 84% becomes 84/100. Then reduce: $\frac{84}{100} = \frac{42}{50} = \frac{21}{25}$*

From a fraction to a decimal
>Multiply the fraction by a number over itself (this is the same as multiplying by 1—it doesn't change the value of the fraction) in order to get the denominator to equal 100, 1000, or another multiple of 100. Then write the numerator by itself, followed by a decimal point. The number of zeros in the denominator will tell you how many places to the left to move the decimal point.
>>*Example: the fraction $\frac{13}{20}$ should be multiplied by $\frac{5}{5}$ to create $\frac{65}{100}$. 65 is the number to use for the decimal, and the two zeroes in the denominator mean that the decimal should be moved two places to the left: 0.65*

From a fraction to a percent
>Follow the steps to convert from a fraction to a decimal above, and then move the decimal point back two places to the right afterward.
>>*Example: the fraction $\frac{2}{5}$ becomes $\frac{40}{100}$, which converts to 0.4 or 40%*

If you want additional practice with these conversions, check out the math drills in the previous chapter.

17. Evaluate the relationship between two variables

When two variables have a correlative relationship, it means that one of the variables (the input, or independent variable) affects the other (the output, or dependent variable). Two common types of relationships are tested on the new SAT: ***direct variation*** between two variables and ***inverse variation***. Understanding the difference between them is key to evaluating their inputs and outputs. Here they are presented one at a time:

Direct variation

In this type of variable relationship, the independent variable has a direct effect upon the dependent variable; that means that **as the inputs increase, the outputs increase** at a constant rate. Another way of looking at a direct variation is the equation $y = kx$, where x is the input, y is the output, and k is the constant.

You might be thinking that $y = kx$ looks like a linear function, and you're absolutely right! If you were to graph a direct variation on the coordinate plane, it would be a straight line, and k would be the slope.

Direct variations can be seen in questions asking about constant rates, such as:

> *Craig is a counselor at a summer day camp with weekly sessions, and he puts together identical welcome bags for his new campers each Monday. Last Monday he needed 36 fun-size candy bars for his 12 campers. How many candy bars will Craig need this Monday if he's expecting 15 campers?*

To solve a problem like this, you can begin by identifying the variables and the constant. The number of campers is the ***input***, and the total number of candy bars is the ***output***, because the number of campers determines the number of candy bars Craig will need.

The welcome bags are identical, meaning that the number of candy bars per bag remains ***constant***. Your constant is a rate—a giveaway that this is a ***direct*** variation.

Since you are given the input and output for last week, you can put them into the equation $y = kx$ to solve for the constant: $36 = k * 12$, so $k = 3$.

Once you know the constant, you can plug it into the equation with the new input (15 campers) to solve for the new output: $y = 3 * 15 = 45$. Craig will need 45 candy bars this Monday!

Inverse variation

In this relationship the independent variable has an inverse effect upon the dependent variable; that means that *as the inputs increase, the outputs decrease* according to a constant. Another way of looking at an inverse variation is the equation $y = \frac{k}{x}$, where x is the input, y is the output, and k is the constant. You can see how this equation works because as x increases—and you divide the constant by larger numbers—the resulting y values will come out smaller.

Examples of inverse variations can be seen in questions where variables are divided out of a constant, like the common equation $time = \frac{distance}{rate}$. In that equation the rate of speed at which you travel a constant distance inversely affects the time it takes to travel (i.e., the greater your speed, the less time it takes). Here's another example:

> Zoe is baking cookies for a party. She has enough dough to make 24 cookies, weighing 3 ounces each. However, several more friends RSVP at the last minute, and Zoe realizes she needs 36 cookies instead. How many ounces should each cookie be?

Again, identify the variables and constant: the **input** is the number of cookies, the **output** is the weight of each cookie, and the **constant** is the dough. You can tell this is an **inverse** relationship because the constant will be divided by the input.

Use the equation $y = \frac{k}{x}$ to find the constant: $3 = \frac{k}{24}$, so $k = 72$.

Zoe has 72 ounces of cookie dough altogether, so if you divide that constant by the new input, you'll have the new output: $y = \frac{72}{36} = 2$.

The new cookies will need to be 2 ounces each.

18. Evaluate irregular functions

Occasionally the SAT includes a function with no rhyme or reason to it—an irregular function. When you see a function that is not linear or exponential (quadratic, cubic, etc.), don't panic! The question will not ask you for an equation when there is none to be had. Instead, the question might ask you about the **qualitative behavior** of the graph, which just means that you must observe information, such as the function's domain and range, maximums and minimums, and other noteworthy characteristics. Consider this question:

In the graph of f(x) shown below, for how many values does f(x) equal 3?

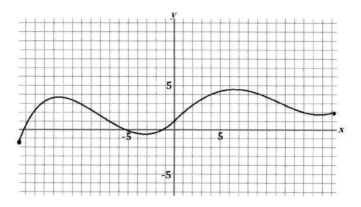

So what does this question really want to know? The number of values for which *f(x)* (the *y*-coordinate) equals 3. In other words, how many points on this function have a *y*-value of 3?

You can handle that! Locate the mark on the *y*-axis that represents 3, and then trace it in both directions. Circle anywhere the function crosses *y* = 3.

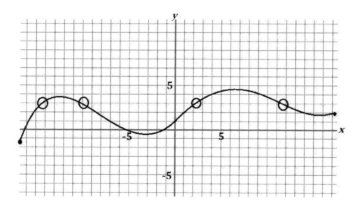

The circles make it clear that the function's *y*-values equal 3 at four distinct points. There's your answer!

19. Evaluate function transformations

Transformations are changes made to functions by performing algebraic operations upon the function's "rules": adding to or subtracting from the function's inputs or outputs, multiplying or dividing the slope, or even multiplying the whole function by a negative to "reverse" it. These transformations are visible on the coordinate plane when transformed functions are graphed. The most common transformations are *translations* and *reflections*.

A *translation* is a "slide" of a function, in which the inputs or outputs (or both) are moved from their original positions. For example, you might be given the following graph of irregular function $g(x)$ and asked to select the answer choice that represents $g(x-1)+2$.

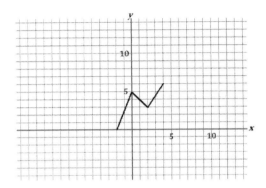

Here is a straightforward way to remember how translations work: If the value change to the function is *inside* the parentheses, it affects the *inputs* (or *x*-values) of the function. If the value change is *outside* the parentheses, it affects the function's *outputs* (or *y*-values).

There is an important "trick" to that rule: Addition and subtraction inside the parentheses cause the function to move in the *opposite* directions of what you might expect.

For example, translating the function $g(x)$ into $g(x+1)$ means that every point on the function's graph shifts 1 unit to the left (towards the negatives), and $g(x-1)$ shifts everything 1 unit to the right (towards the positives).

Changes outside the parentheses move just as you'd expect; $g(x)+2$ moves everything up 2 units, for instance.

For the function $g(x)$ shown in the graph above, then, the graph of $g(x-1)+2$ would look like the graph at the right.

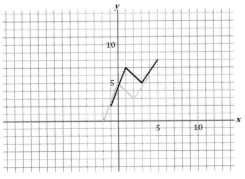

See how every point on the original graph (shown in light gray) has been shifted 1 unit to the right and 2 units up? The function's graph has "slid" to represent the translation.

Just like translations, *reflections*—mirror images—of functions over the axes depend on where the change happens—inside or outside the parentheses. For any function $f(x)$, the reflection $f(-x)$ reverses all inputs, or *x*-coordinates. This reversal creates a ***horizontal*** reflection (over the *y*-axis). For the same function, the reflection $-f(x)$ reverses all outputs, or *y*-coordinates, which creates a ***vertical*** reflection (over the *x*-axis).

20. Evaluate charts, graphs, and written data

The new SAT has an increased focus upon data analysis and interpretation. Data can be presented in a number of ways on the Math Test: circle graphs (also known as pie charts), line graphs, bar graphs, scatterplots (with or without a line of best fit), and data tables.

No matter what type of data you are given on the test, you should always take a moment for each of the following quick steps:

1. Determine *what* is being measured by the data presentation (i.e., the variables).
2. Check *how* it is being measured (i.e., what units are used).
3. Assess *where* the data goes. Are there any trends or patterns in the data?

Stopping to check these things first before diving into a question will help you to know what you're dealing with, as well as what information you have available. Now let's briefly review what these data presentation types look like and why they are used.

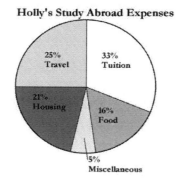

Circle Graph: Also known as a pie chart, a circle graph looks like a pie cut into wedges. Each wedge is used to represent a part (usually a percent) of the whole, so circle graphs are often used to measure ratios. A sample circle graph is given at the left.

Line Graph: A line graph shows points of data on a coordinate plane with line segments connecting the dots. The lines are used to show increases and decreases between the points, often over a period of time. Sometimes two line graphs will be put on the same plane—for instance, monthly profits for two companies—in order to get a side-by-side comparison. A sample line graph is given at the right.

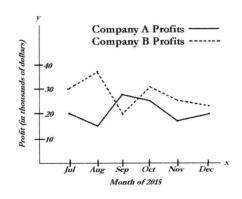

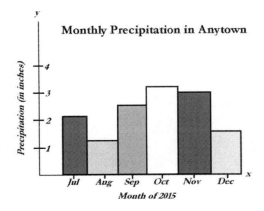

Bar Graph: A bar graph shows amounts or discrete measurements, such as temperatures, on a coordinate plane with a bar for each measurement. Bar graphs are useful for calculating sums and differences of amounts. A sample bar graph is shown at the left.

Scatterplot: A scatterplot is a representation of points of data on the coordinate plane, in order to see the output for each input. A ***line of best fit*** estimates the slope (or output per input) of the plotted points. A question might ask you to determine a line of best fit; to do this, evaluate the slope between several pairs of points and average them, then estimate the output when the input is 0. A sample scatterplot is shown at the right.

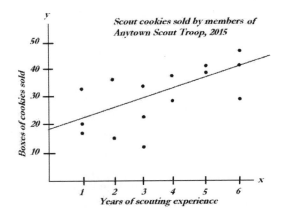

Pairs of Shoes Sold at Sal's Shoe Store

	Week 1	Week 2
Sneakers	15	17
Flats	11	9
Heels	18	15
Boots	12	16

Data Table: A table is another way of representing data; it shows each point just like a scatterplot, but instead of a visual representation on the coordinate plane, a table lists the points by variable or category. A sample table is given at the left.

If you are given data in a table format, but you are more of a visual learner, then don't hesitate to "reformat" the data in a way that is useful for you.

The data in the table above, for instance, could also be easily represented in a bar graph with two bars for each type of shoe sold (one bar for Week 1 and one for Week 2). Likewise, if you prefer the precision and list-like structure of a data table, you could quickly translate the line chart on the previous page into a table.

As long as you are consistent with the data, you can look at it in any format you choose, and it's worth taking an extra 30 seconds to change things up if it will help you get the question right!

21. Use sample data to make inferences about a population

When you are given sample data on the new SAT, such as those shown in the examples for the previous concept, you might be asked to make ***inferences*** about the population or trends (patterns) in the data. You might recall from the Reading Test chapter that an inference is a reasonable conclusion based upon the given facts. With that in mind, start with the facts you're given by the question. Remember these three steps to take first:

1. Determine *what* variables are being measured by the data presentation. In a graph the independent variable is on the *x*-axis, and the dependent variable on the *y*-axis.

2. Check *how* it is being measured (i.e., what units are used).

3. Assess *where* the data goes. Are there any trends or patterns in the data?

Let's work through those steps for a practice problem. Try this example:

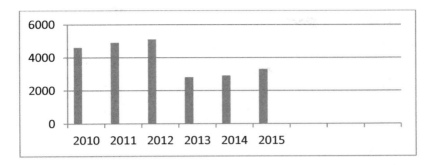

The bar graph above represents the annual harvest of apples (in tons) by Simon's Apple Orchard between 2010 and 2015. Which of the following can be inferred from the information shown?

    (A) *The orchard increased in production every year.*
    (B) *The 2013 growing season faced some kind of misfortune or loss of harvest, followed by a rebound.*
    (C) *The 2013 growing season marked the beginning of a steady decline.*
    (D) *The 2016 harvest will be stronger than the 2015 harvest.*

Before jumping into the answer choices, go through the steps to know what you're looking for:

Step 1: What is being measured?   The annual harvest of apples in an orchard.

Step 2: How is it being measured?   The number of tons of apples (dependent variable) is measured by year (independent variable).

Step 3: Where is the data going?   Trends in the data: increases over the first three years, then a sharp drop in 2013, and then increases again.

With that information in mind, now look at the answers. *(A)* is out, because the harvest does not increase every year. *(B)* is a reasonable inference based on the trends in the data. Check the last two to be sure. *(C)* is false, because the harvest increased in 2014 and 2015. *(D)* is tricky because it is an **assumption**; it could be true, but we can't reasonably depend on it. What if whatever happened in 2013 happens again in 2016? Therefore, *(B)* has to be the answer!

22. Use descriptive statistics to evaluate data

Statistics are among the most useful math topics for "real life" after the SAT: you see them in sports, political polls, weather forecasts, and even your own grade point average. The new SAT addresses the five most common elements of descriptive statistics, also known as the *Five Ms*:

Cecil's Tips to Stay Sharp

Minimum	*The smallest value included in the data set.*
Maximum	*The largest value included in the data set. The difference between the maximum and minimum is called the **range** of the set.*
Mean	*Also called arithmetic mean or average, this is the sum of all values in the set, divided by the number of values in the set.*
Median	*The middle value when the set's values are placed in numeric order. If the set has an even number of values, then the median is the average of the two middle values.*
Mode	*The value that appears most frequently in the data set. There can be multiple modes, or no mode at all, depending on whether the values in a set have any "repeats."*

Note that with the mean, or average, you can use the formula $average = \frac{sum\ of\ terms}{number\ of\ terms}$ *to solve for any of those three components if you only know the other two. For instance:*

$$avg = \frac{80}{15}, so\ avg = 5.3\overline{3}$$

$$60 = \frac{sum}{4}, so\ 240 = sum$$

Consider the following data set, made up of a student's quiz grades in chemistry class:

95, 89, 93, 76, 84, 96, 81, 93, 79, 84

Let's practice finding the Five Ms for this data set:

Minimum   *The lowest score is a 76.*

Maximum   *The highest score is a 96.*

Mean   Assuming that these ten grades are weighted equally, we would add them all up (870) and divide by ten to find a mean grade of 87.

Median   This takes a little more legwork because the grades are not in numeric order. Rearrange them in order—76, 79, 81, 84, 84, 89, 93, 93, 95, 96. The middle two values in this ten-value set are 84 and 89, so we would average them (add up and divide by two) to get a median of 86.5.

Mode   This set has two modes—84 and 93 each appear twice, while each of the other values appears only once.

23. Work with weighted averages

A weighted average (arithmetic mean) is composed of terms that are not all equal in importance (or weight). You might have seen these before in classes; for example, if your research paper is worth 20 percent of your overall grade, and the final exam is worth 40 percent, then they are **weighted** differently, and a good score on the final will do more for your overall grade than a good score on the paper.

The way to handle a question like this is to take the weights back out of it, by totaling up the sums of the different components and dividing by the total number of terms. Let's practice this concept with a question:

> *During the annual Scouts cookie sale, Troop A's 12 members each sold an average of 40 boxes of cookies. The 8 members of Troop B sold an average of 80 boxes each. What was the average number of boxes sold by Troops A and B combined?*

The catch on a problem like this is that you can't just average 40 and 80 (though you can bet that would be an answer choice), because more Scouts sold an average of 40. Troop A is weighted more heavily here than Troop B. Here's how to take the weight back out of it:

Troop A's 12 members averaged 40 boxes each. $40 \; boxes = \frac{sum}{12 \; members}$

That means that Troop A sold a sum of 480 boxes of cookies.

Likewise, Troop B's 8 members averaged 80 boxes each. $80 = \frac{sum}{8}$

Therefore, Troop B sold a sum of 640 boxes.

Now that we know the sum for each troop, we can total them and divide by the total number of members to **un-weight** the problem and make a new average:

$$\text{average of both troops} = \frac{(480 + 640) \text{ boxes of cookies}}{20 \text{ members}}$$

$$\text{average} = \frac{1120}{20} = 56 \text{ boxes per member}$$

This un-weighting approach also works very well for averaging rates, such as miles per hour. Consider a question like this:

> On Friday Jim drove 200 miles from Pittsburgh to Columbus at an average speed of 60 miles per hour. On Monday he took the same route back at an average speed of 40 mph, thanks to a bunch of construction zones. What was Jim's average speed for the roundtrip in miles per hour?

Again, we can't just average 60 and 40. Why not? Because Jim went the same distance each way. He spent *more time* traveling at the slower speed, so 40 mph is weighted more heavily. In order to calculate the roundtrip average speed in miles per hour, we need to find the total number of miles and divide by the total number of hours—that will take the weighting out of the question.

$$\frac{200 \text{ miles}}{60 \text{ miles per hour}} = 3\frac{1}{3} \text{ hours for the first trip}$$

$$\frac{200 \text{ miles}}{40 \text{ miles per hour}} = 5 \text{ hours for the return trip}$$

With the total distance and total time, we can now calculate the average speed!

$$\frac{(200+200) \text{ miles}}{\left(3\frac{1}{3}+5\right) \text{ hours}} = \frac{400 \text{ miles}}{8\frac{1}{3} \text{ hours}} = 48 \text{ miles per hour}$$

24. Use averages to find a missing number

The formula $average = \frac{sum\ of\ terms}{number\ of\ terms}$ can be used in many helpful ways, as seen above. One way you might not have considered using it is to find "missing" numbers. For instance, consider this problem:

> *The average of Kara's ten fastest recorded times for the 100-meter sprint is 16.2 seconds. The average of her nine fastest recorded times for the sprint is 15.8 seconds. What is the slowest of Kara's ten fastest times?*

This might seem like you weren't given enough information, but you were. We know Kara's averages for her top ten times and her top nine times, so the difference between the two will be the missing (slowest) time. Just like with the weighted averages discussed above, take it back to the totals:

$16.2\ seconds = \frac{sum\ of\ 10\ times}{10}$

$162\ seconds = sum\ of\ 10\ times$

$15.8\ seconds = \frac{sum\ of\ 9\ times}{9}$

$142.2\ seconds = sum\ of\ 9\ times$

$(sum\ of\ 10) - (sum\ of\ 9) = 162 - 142.2 = 19.8\ seconds$

Make sense? By using what we know about averages, we can calculate sums including and excluding the number we're looking for. Then all we have to do is take the difference between them to deduce the missing number!

25. Calculate standard deviation

The new SAT includes a previously excluded statistical measure called ***standard deviation***. This is a measure of distance from the mean that helps to illustrate how spread-out or condensed a data set is. Standard deviation might seem like a pain, but it is something that you will see again in college, especially if you're considering a major that involves any kind of social or physical science. It's well worth your time to learn about it now!

Standard deviation is a measure of variance, or distance, from the mean within a given dataset. The greater the variance in data, the greater the standard deviation. The Greek letter σ (lowercase sigma) represents standard deviation. Here is the formula for standard deviation:

$$\sigma = \sqrt{\frac{\Sigma(x - \bar{x})^2}{n}}$$

No getting around it—that looks *horrible*. But by understanding what the components mean and how they work together, rather than just trying to memorize this mess of variables, you will be able to handle any standard deviation question that the new SAT might throw at you! So let's break this down:

x is a given value within the dataset.

$\bar{x}$ is the mean of the dataset.

Σ (uppercase Greek letter sigma) is the symbol for "sum."

n is the number of values in the dataset.

Here's how you use those pieces to calculate standard deviation:

1. Calculate the mean: $\bar{x}$.
2. Find the difference between each value and the mean, and square the differences: $(x - \bar{x})^2$.
3. Find the mean of the squared differences: $\frac{\Sigma(x-\bar{x})^2}{n}$. This fancy notation just means that you are adding them up and dividing by the number of values in the set—in other words, simply finding an average.
4. The square root of that mean is the standard deviation!

Not quite as bad as it looked at first. Still pretty messy, but if you can do it in four steps, it can't be *that* dreadful, right?

…Right?

Try it out on this sample dataset!

{86, 91, 79, 97, 85, 74, 90, 94}

1. Calculate the mean: $\frac{86+91+79+97+85+74+90+94}{8} = 87$.
2. Find the difference between each value and the mean, and square the differences.

Value (x)	Difference between value and mean ($x - \bar{x}$)	$(x - \bar{x})^2$
74	-13	169
79	-8	64
85	-2	4
86	-1	1
90	3	9
91	4	16
95	8	64
97	10	100

3. Find the mean of the squared differences: $\frac{169+64+4+1+9+16+64+100}{8} = 53.375$.
4. Take the square root of the mean: $\sqrt{53.375} = 7.306$.

7.306 is the standard deviation of the dataset.

26. Create equivalent polynomial expressions and ratios

Polynomials can be tricky to navigate on the SAT—some students are just learning to work with them, and other students may have seen them awhile back in another math class. Either way, whether they are fresh in your mind or dusty from yesteryear, polynomials have several rules that you'll need to remember.

Polynomials are literally "multi-termed" algebraic expressions. A polynomial is composed of algebraic expressions that have been multiplied together, so its x will always be taken to an exponential power greater than 1.

The most common polynomial that you'll need to work with is a *quadratic*, which contains x^2 but no higher exponents.

If you see algebraic terms multiplied together in an expression or equation, you can multiply out the terms one by one and combine like terms to convert the whole thing into a quadratic in **standard form**: $f(x) = ax^2 + bx + c$.

Cecil's Tips to Stay Sharp

Read through to the end of this concept for a light at the end of the tunnel—a shortcut for dealing with polynomials that will have you singing and dancing with relief! (In your head, of course. You're unfortunately not allowed to sing and dance during the SAT.)

The systematic way to remember how to multiply out the terms and get a quadratic expression is called **FOIL**, which stands for **First** terms, **Outside** terms, **Inside** terms, **Last** terms. To get to standard form, you'll need to multiply each pair of terms and then just add them up.

Let's practice FOIL-ing with the following equation:

$f(x) = (x + 4)(x - 3)$ *Start by multiplying the **First** terms: $x * x = x^2$.*

*Then multiply the **Outside** terms: $x * -3 = -3x$.*

*Next, multiply the **Inside** terms: $4 * x = 4x$.*

*Finally, multiply the **Last** terms: $4 * -3 = -12$.*

$f(x) = x^2 - 3x + 4x - 12$ *All the terms are in place; now just combine like terms.*

$f(x) = x^2 + x - 12$ *That's it! Now the whole thing is pieced into a polynomial.*

FOIL is a great quick method to convert from a product of algebraic terms to a polynomial in standard form. It will work for other polynomials besides quadratics, too; just make sure that each term of the first expression gets multiplied with each term of the second expression. Here is an example of FOIL, so to speak, to get from two different algebraic terms to a higher polynomial:

$f(x) = (x + 2)(x^2 + 3x + 4)$ *Multiply **x** by each term in the second set of parentheses, then multiply **2** by each term in the second set.*

$f(x) = x^3 + 3x^2 + 4x + 2x^2 + 6x + 8$ *Combine like terms.*

$f(x) = x^3 + 5x^2 + 10x + 8$ *You now have a **cubic** function!*

If on the other hand you have a quadratic function that you need to convert back to a product of algebraic factors, you can also **reverse-FOIL**. This takes a little more critical thinking, but it's still systematic. To reverse-FOIL (or factor) a quadratic, you need to consider the values of b and c in $f(x) = ax^2 + bx + c$. When taken back to its factors, the function $f(x) = ax^2 + bx + c$ will need to look like this:

$f(x) = (ax + something)(x + something)$

The two somethings will need to *add up* to the value of *b* and *multiply* to the value of *c*. For example, in the function $f(x) = x^2 - 7x + 12$, the two values that will go in the parentheses will need to add up to -7 and multiply to 12. To start finding the values, it works well to write the equation with blanks for what you don't yet know.

$f(x) = (x\_\_\_)(x\_\_\_)$ *Now think how 12 could be factored: 1 and 12; 2 and 6; 3 and 4. Of those numbers, 3 and 4 are the factors that would add up to 7, so we can fill in 3 and 4 as the missing values.*

$f(x) = (x\_3)(x\_4)$ *The only thing that's left to determine is whether the signs should be positive or negative. Since the numbers need to add up to -7 but multiply to create a positive, they should both be negative.*

$f(x) = (x - 3)(x - 4)$ *That is the factored version of the polynomial! You can check it by using FOIL to work your way back to the unfactored equation and making sure it matches the original.*

If you're asked to divide a quadratic polynomial like $x^2 + 3x + 2$ by a binomial like $x + 2$, this type of factoring will work beautifully. After all, you've already been given one of the terms! But if the Math Test asks you to divide $x^3 + 5x^2 + 10x + 8$ by $x + 2$, then reverse-FOIL is not going to cut it. There are at least two ways to tackle a problem like this, though, so don't worry!

The first is good old long division. Let's work through the steps of long division to solve the problem above:

$x + 2 \overline{\smash{)}x^3 + 5x^2 + 10x + 8}$ *Start by setting up the expressions in a division "house" with the **divisor** (the expression you're dividing by) on the outside.*

$\begin{array}{r} x^2 \\ x+2 \overline{\smash{)}x^3 + 5x^2 + 10x + 8} \\ x^3 + 2x^2 \end{array}$ *Compare the first term of the divisor to the first term of the **dividend** (the expression being divided). What do you need to multiply the divisor's first term by to make them equal? x^2, which you then multiply by **both** terms of the divisor. Write the results underneath the corresponding terms.*

$$\begin{array}{r}x^2\\ x+2\,{\overline{\smash{\big)}\,x^3+5x^2+10x+8}}\\ \underline{-(x^3+2x^2)}\Downarrow\\ \varnothing\quad 3x^2+10x\end{array}$$

Subtract the results you wrote from the terms above them. The first terms should cancel each other out, and the second term will be the one you multiply into next. Drop down the next term of the dividend (as shown by the arrow) to keep working with two terms at a time.

$$\begin{array}{r}x^2+3x\\ x+2\,{\overline{\smash{\big)}\,x^3+5x^2+10x+8}}\\ \underline{-(x^3+2x^2)}\\ \varnothing\quad 3x^2+10x\\ \underline{-(3x^2+6x)}\\ \varnothing\quad4x+8\end{array}$$

Follow the same steps you took before. What do you need to multiply x by to get $3x^2$? $3x$. Then you multiply $3x$ by both x and 2 and put the results under the corresponding terms. Subtract the results from the terms above them to cancel out the first term. Drop down the next term. You're almost there!

$$\begin{array}{r}x^2+3x+4\\ x+2\,{\overline{\smash{\big)}\,x^3+5x^2+10x+8}}\\ \underline{-(x^3+2x^2)}\\ \varnothing\quad 3x^2+10x\\ \underline{-(3x^2+6x)}\\ \varnothing\quad4x+8\\ \underline{-(4x+8)}\\ \varnothing\quad\varnothing\end{array}$$

All right, run through those steps one more time. Find the term you need on top, multiply it by the terms of your divisor, and subtract the results to cancel out.

Since both terms cancel out this time, you know that you are done and that there is no remainder. $x^3+5x^2+10x+8$ divided by $x+2$ equals x^2+3x+4.

Well, that was a mental workout, wasn't it? Long division takes a little elbow grease, but it is definitely worth it to keep this strategy in your back pocket in case you ever need it.

The other route to the answer, though, is the shortcut that will have you breaking into a mental happy dance. You can use this shortcut whenever the question looks something like this:

The expression $\dfrac{x^3+5x^2+10x+8}{x+2}$ *is equivalent to which of the following?*

(A) $x^2 + 5x + 10$
(B) $x^2 - 5x - 8$
(C) $x^2 + 3x + 4$
(D) $x^2 + 3x - 5$

What can you do with a question that has all its answer choices in terms of a variable? **Work the Question**! Remember that strategy described on page 113? It works beautifully to turn complex algebra like this into arithmetic that you could even solve without a calculator. Choose an easy-to-work-with number, like 2, to substitute in for x in the original expression.

$\dfrac{(2)^3+5(2)^2+10(2)+8}{2+2}$ *Simplify the expression until you have a numeric equivalent for it when $x = 2$.*

$\dfrac{8+20+20+8}{4} = \dfrac{56}{4} = 14$ *So when $x = 2$, the given expression is equal to 14. Now just plug 2 in for x in each of the answer choices and see which one also equals 14.*

(A) $x^2 + 5x + 10$ $4 + 10 + 10 = 24$
(B) $x^2 - 5x - 8$ $4 - 10 - 8 = -14$
(C) $x^2 + 3x + 4$ $4 + 6 + 4 =$ **14**   *This is the only answer that matches!*
(D) $x^2 + 3x - 5$ $4 + 6 - 5 = 5$

Now, is that a good way to outsmart polynomials or what? With Working the Question, long division, and factoring at your disposal, you will be able to handle any polynomial expressions you see on the test. Go ahead—if nobody's watching, do a little happy dance. We won't tell.

27. Factor polynomials to solve for zeros

When set equal to 0 or $f(x)$, a quadratic expression becomes an exponential equation or function and can be solved for its *zeros*, meaning the *x*-values that will produce *y*-values of 0 when plugged into the function. If you were to graph a quadratic function, its zeros would be the points at which the graph crossed the *x*-axis.

To use factoring to solve for the zeros of a quadratic equation, you will need to put the equation into its **standard form**: $f(x) = ax^2 + bx + c$. When you are solving for zeros, $f(x)$ can also be replaced with 0 because you're looking for inputs that will produce an output of 0.

Once you have a quadratic equation in standard form, you should factor, or reverse-FOIL, the polynomial into two terms with no exponents. Reverse-FOIL was discussed in the previous topic, but to reiterate: You are taking the equation from $f(x) = ax^2 + bx + c$ to $f(x) = (ax + something)(x + something)$. The two somethings should *add up* to the value of *b* and *multiply* to the value of *c*.

Let's practice with this equation:

$f(x) = x^2 + 5x + 6$ *Rewrite the function in factored form with blanks.*

$f(x) = (x\_\_\_)(x\_\_\_)$ *Now, what could add up to 5 and multiply to 6? 2 and 3!*

$f(x) = (x + 2)(x + 3)$ *To check your answer, you can FOIL the terms back out to make sure they equal the original equation.*

$x = -2, -3$ *-2 and -3 are the zeros of this function, because when you plug either of them in for x, the function's output will equal 0.*

If you are using this approach and you ever have trouble finding numbers that add up and multiply together properly, don't worry; just refer to Concept #11: "Work with divisibility: factors, multiples, and primes." You can make a **T-chart** for the value of *c* to list its factors in pairs, and then look for the pair that sums to the value of *b*.

Note that when you're working with quadratics in the form $ax^2 + bx + c$, *a* will often equal 1. That's the ideal situation for solving by factoring, since you don't have to worry about how *a* affects the factors of *b* and *c*. If *a* equals something else, though, or if factoring is just not working out on that particular equation, you might want to use another method… like the ones in the next concept!

28. Solve a quadratic equation by using the Quadratic Formula or graphing

Factoring a quadratic equation in the form $f(x) = ax^2 + bx + c$ is one way to solve it (find the zeros), but what if you have a crazy value for a that makes it hard to factor? Why, use the **Quadratic Formula**, of course!

The Quadratic Formula is a method of calculating the zeros of a quadratic function (the points at which the function's outputs equal 0, or where it crosses the x-axis). The great thing about using the Quadratic Formula is that you just plug in the coefficients from your quadratic equation and then just follow the order of operations to get to your answers. It looks like this:

$$x = \frac{-b \pm \sqrt{b^2 - 4ac}}{2a}$$

Yikes! Yes, there's a lot going on in there, and even if you've already learned it in math class, it can be easy to forget all the pieces.

… Or can it?

If you weren't lucky enough to have a creative math teacher who taught you the Quadratic Formula using the world's best mnemonic device (memory trick), then feel lucky now, because we're going to let you in on it.

Sing the following to the tune of "Pop Goes the Weasel":

X equals negative B,

Plus or minus square root of

B squared minus 4AC

All over 2A.

That is the Quadratic Formula! Set to a memorable tune, it becomes much easier to keep track of all the elements. If you haven't yet memorized the Quadratic Formula, serenade this page with musical renditions of it until you know it by heart. When you need it on the SAT, you'll be glad you did!

Using the Quadratic Formula will also helpfully let you know if a quadratic function has *no* real solutions (zeros). If that is the case you'll end up with a negative value under a radical (an imaginary number) as part of your answer.

If you are pressed for time or would rather see a visual representation of the quadratic function you're working with, then using your graphing calculator (such as a TI-84 or TI-84 Plus) is a great way to visually evaluate a quadratic function. It also can provide you with the zeros if you follow these steps:

1. Type the equation into your graphing calculator and view the graph.
2. Adjust the window and scale of your graph as needed.
3. Press the "CALC" button and select "ZERO."
4. Follow the prompts to select points on the graph and press "Enter." The calculator will report the value of one zero.
5. Repeat steps 3 and 4 to find the other zero.

Just like using the Quadratic Formula, graphing a quadratic equation will let you know if it has no real solutions (zeros). If that is the case, the graph will not cross the x-axis at any point.

Again, technology can be very helpful—but it's also good to know the "old-fashioned" methods in case you need them. With *factoring*, the **Quadratic Formula**, and *calculator* methods at your disposal, you'll be able to evaluate any quadratic functions on the new SAT!

29. Evaluate a quadratic or other function graph

Questions that ask you to interpret regular function graphs typically come in two forms. Either they give you an equation and ask you which answer choice is an accurate graph of that equation, or they give you a graph and ask you which answer choice is an accurate equation for that graph.

Recognizing what *parent functions* look like will help you here. Here are several common parent functions:

Linear: $f(x) = x$ **Absolute Value**: $f(x) = |x|$ **Quadratic**: $f(x) = x^2$

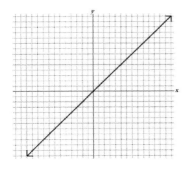 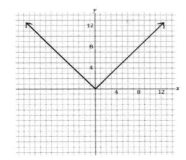 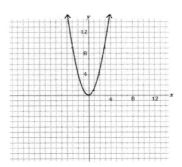

Note that linear and absolute functions look alike, except that negative x-values produce positive y-values in absolute functions; remember, this is because absolute value means "distance from zero," and distance cannot be negative.

For a linear or absolute value function, the slope and *y*-intercept will determine the placement of the function on the coordinate plane. Consider the standard forms $f(x) = mx + b$ and $f(x) = |mx + b|$. The greater the slope (value of *m*), the more steeply the line will graph. The *y*-intercept (value of *b*) sets where the graph will cross the axis.

The system is a little more complicated for quadratic functions. The **leading coefficient**, or *a*-value in the standard form $f(x) = ax^2 + bx + c$, tells you the most about the function's graph. If *a* is positive, the parabola will open upward, and if *a* is negative, the parabola will open downward.

Also, just like a linear function, the greater the value of *a*, the more steep (or narrow) the parabola will look.

That information alone will usually be enough to tell you which graph or function is the right answer. However, occasionally functions will be *transformed* through *translation* (a slide) or *reflection* (a mirror image) on the coordinate plane. For a review of how transformations work, refer to Concept #19, "Evaluate function transformations."

30. Recognize and work with special polynomials

There are a few commonly tested polynomials that are considered "special" because of their factoring properties. You don't have to memorize their standard and factored forms, but it certainly wouldn't hurt. If you recognize one on the test and can quickly convert it to another form, it could save you precious time to spend on something else. So check them out!

Squared Sum: $\qquad (a+b)^2 = a^2 + 2ab + b^2$

Squared Difference: $\qquad (a-b)^2 = a^2 - 2ab + b^2$

Difference of Squares: $\qquad a^2 - b^2 = (a+b)(a-b)$

31. Apply properties of exponents

Exponents show up in several forms on the Math Test. If you're feeling a little unsure on the fundamentals or would just like a brush-up, then review the following properties below. You can find additional practice with the exponents drill in the previous chapter.

Multiplying and dividing exponents

When an exponent is multiplied by another exponent with the same base (e.g., $10^4 * 10^5$), the powers can be added together in the product (e.g., $10^{4+5} = 10^9$). Likewise, when an exponent is divided by another exponent with the same base, the powers can be subtracted from one another in the quotient (e.g., $\frac{4^8}{4^5} = 4^{(8-5)} = 4^3$).

Raising an exponent to another exponent

When a number is raised to one power and then raised to another, the powers can be multiplied together, such as $(5^3)^2 = 5^{3*2} = 5^6$.

Properties of special exponents

Any number raised to the power of 1 equals itself: $x^1 = x$

Any ratio raised to a power equals the numerator raised to that power over the denominator raised to that power: $(\frac{3}{4})^2 = \frac{9}{16}$

Any negative number raised to an even power becomes positive.

Cecil's Tips to Stay Sharp

It pays to be flexible with exponents on the SAT, like when you see something like this: $4^2 * 2^3 = 2^n$. Since they don't have the same base, you can't simply add the powers together. But if you notice that 4 equals 2^2, this equation quickly becomes more solvable! $(2^2)^2 = 2^4$, and so $2^4 * 2^3 = 2^{(4+3)} = 2^7$. Because $2^7 = 2^n$, $n = 7$.

Raised to an odd power, the number stays negative: $(-3)^2 = -3 * -3 = 9$
$(-3)^3 = -3 * -3 * -3 = -27$

Any number raised to the power of 0 equals 1: $x^0 = 1$

Any number raised to a negative exponent equals the reciprocal of that exponent: $x^{-n} = \frac{1}{x^n}$

Any number raised to a rational (or fractional) exponent has a power and a root. The numerator of the exponent is the power, and the denominator is the root: $x^{\left(\frac{a}{b}\right)} = \sqrt[b]{x^a}$

> *(A good way to remember that last rule is that **roots** are on the bottom of a tree, just like the bottom number in a rational exponent represents the root.)*

32. Work with radical expressions and equations

A radical, or "root," can be thought of as the opposite of a power. It is expressed by the symbol $\sqrt{}$.

In sentence form: *If x squared is equal to y, then the square root of y is x (or –x).*

In equation form: *If $x^2 = y$, then $\sqrt{y} = \pm x$.*

For example, $5^2 = 25$ and $(-5)^2 = 25$, so $\sqrt{25}$ is equal to both 5 and -5.

The SAT rewards test takers who can be flexible with roots and radicals by converting and simplifying them where appropriate. The quickest radical to simplify is $\sqrt{x^2} = \pm x$, and you can perform that simplification whenever you see a perfect square value under a square root. Likewise, $\sqrt[3]{x^3}$ can be simplified to x, and $\sqrt[4]{x^4}$ to $\pm x$, and so on.

Why doesn't $\sqrt[3]{x^3}$ simplify to $\pm x$ like the other two expressions? Because when something is raised to an odd power, there's no opportunity for the negatives to cancel each other out. $(-2)^2 = -2 * -2 = 4$, so $\sqrt{4} = \pm 2$, but $(-2)^3 = -2 * -2 * -2 = -8$, so $\sqrt[3]{-8}$ only equals -3.

Keep in mind that *you don't need to have perfect squares under square roots* in order to simplify them. Instead, you can simplify out any factor of a number under a square root, as long as the factor is a perfect square.

For instance, look at $\sqrt{48}$. The whole number is not a perfect square, but it can be factored into $\sqrt{16*3}$, or $\sqrt{4^2 * 3}$. The final step is to pull out the perfect square: $\pm 4\sqrt{3}$.

This concept also applies to problems with cube roots and greater roots. You'll just need to pull out factors that are "perfect" for the particular root in that problem: 27, or 3^3, for a cube root; 16, or 2^4, for a 4th root, etc.

Here's one more important reminder about radicals. When you're solving an equation with a square root in it, isolate the radical *before* squaring both sides to simplify. Here's an example to illustrate why:

$3 + \sqrt{2x+6} = -5$ *If you squared both sides here, you'd still have a mess of radicals!*

$\sqrt{2x+6} = -8$ *After subtracting 3 from both sides, the radical is alone.*

$2x + 6 = 64$ *Squaring both sides now turns this into a neat linear equation.*

$2x = 58$ *Follow the order of operations…*

$x = 29$ *And easy-peasy (relatively speaking), there's the answer!*

33. Rationalize a denominator

Rationalizing a denominator is one of those things you hear about in math class that just sounds dreadful, long before you actually learn how to do it.

However, once you actually learn how to do it, rationalizing denominators isn't that bad! It rests on the idea that it is easier to work with fractions divided by rational numbers (preferably integers) than it is to work with fractions divided by wonky things like $\sqrt{15}$.

The three steps you have to take in order to rationalize a denominator are to **recognize it**, **multiply it**, and **simplify it**.

Recognize it: A fraction with a radical (root) in the denominator, such as $\frac{3}{\sqrt{18}}$, must be rationalized. (A fraction with a radical in the numerator only is fine as it is.)

Multiply it: Remember, multiplying a fraction by any value over that same value is just like multiplying by 1; you're not changing the fraction's value, so multiplying is just fine.

With the fraction $\frac{3}{\sqrt{18}}$, you should multiply by $\frac{\sqrt{18}}{\sqrt{18}}$. Why? Because look what happens when you…

Simplify it: Multiplying the numerators and denominators straight across will produce $\frac{3\sqrt{18}}{(\sqrt{18})(\sqrt{18})}$. The denominator simplifies to $\sqrt{18}^2$, or just 18. Hooray, an integer! Then you need to simplify the numerator and put the fraction into lowest terms, like this:

$$\frac{3\sqrt{18}}{18} = \frac{3\sqrt{9*2}}{18} = \frac{3*3\sqrt{2}}{18} = \frac{9\sqrt{2}}{18} = \frac{\sqrt{2}}{2}$$

In the numerator, the 18 under the radical can be split into 9 (a perfect square) and 2. You take the square root of 9 to bring it out from under the radical as a 3, and then you reduce the fraction. Not that bad, right?

If you want to review how to work with radicals in order to get more comfortable with simplifying expressions like this, then refer to Concept #32: "Work with radical expressions and equations."

34. Evaluate lines and angles in plane geometry

Plane geometry is a concept of two-dimensional measurement—of lines, angles, and shapes that lie on a flat surface. In plane geometry you can measure distance, perimeter (or distance around a figure), area, and angle measure. The next several concepts will review how to calculate these measurements for a variety of figures, but we will start with the basics: lines and angles.

Line: a straight one-dimensional concept with no endpoints. A line has arrows at both ends indicating infinite extension. In the given diagram, n is a line.

Line segment: a piece of a line with discrete endpoints. The length of a line segment is measurable because it is finite. In the given diagram, m and s are line segments.

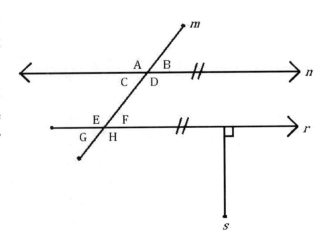

Ray: a piece of a line with one discrete endpoint and one arrow. In other words, a ray starts at a point and extends forever in one direction only.

Midpoint: a point on a line segment that has equal distance from each of the endpoints.

Angle: a figure formed by two rays or line segments that meet at a point (called the *vertex*). The wideness of the angle is measured in degrees, expressed by the symbol °.

Acute angle: an angle measuring less than 90 degrees. In the given diagram, B, C, F, and G are acute angles.

Right angle: an angle measuring 90 degrees, expressed by the square symbol. In the given diagram, the angle formed by line segment *s* and ray *r* is a right angle.

Obtuse angle: an angle measuring greater than 90 but less than 180 degrees. In the given diagram, A, D, E, and H are obtuse angles.

Straight angle: an angle measuring 180 degrees.

Reflex angle: an angle measuring greater than 180 degrees.

Bisect: when an angle is cut in half by an intersecting ray or segment. For instance, a bisected right angle (measuring 90°) would create two angles of 45° each.

Parallel lines: lines, rays, or line segments that run in exactly the same direction and will never intersect. In the figure on the previous page, line *n* and ray *r* are parallel.

Perpendicular lines: lines that intersect or meet at a right angle. In the figure on the previous page, ray *r* and line segment *s* are perpendicular.

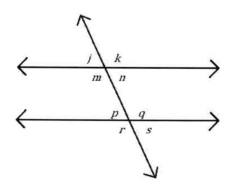

Complementary angles: two angles with degree measurements that add up to 90 degrees (a right angle).

Supplementary angles: two angles with degree measurements that add up to 180 degrees (a straight line). In the figure at the left, angles *j* and *k* are examples of supplementary angles.

Vertical angles: two angles that are across from one another in the intersection of two lines. In the figure at the left, *j* and *n* are examples of vertical angles.

Corresponding angles: two angles that are in the same positions within the intersections between parallel lines and a *transversal* (a line that cuts through both parallel lines). In the figure above, *k* and *q* are examples of corresponding angles.

A good thing to note about those last few definitions is that if you know one angle measure in an intersection, you can quickly find all four—and if you have parallel lines cut by a transversal and are given only one angle measure, you can find all *eight* angles!

In the figure above, for example, suppose angle *j* measured 60°. Angle *j* is vertical to angle *n*, and those two angles correspond to angles *p* and *s* respectively, so all four of those angles must equal 60°. Angle *k* is supplementary to angle *j*, so it must equal 120°; angle *k* is vertical to angle *m*, and those two angles correspond to angles *q* and *r* respectively, so all four of those angles must equal 120°. You can quickly fill in an entire diagram!

35. Measure and evaluate triangles

Of all the shapes in plane (two-dimensional) geometry, triangles are the most commonly tested. They are very systematic, and there are several key theorems and ratios to keep in mind when dealing with them. Here are some definitions to get you started:

Triangle: a polygon (enclosed shape with straight sides) that has three sides and three vertices (angles). The degrees in the angles of a triangle always add up to 180 degrees.

Scalene Triangle: a type of triangle that has three sides of different lengths and three vertices of different measurements. The triangle at the right is an example of a scalene triangle.

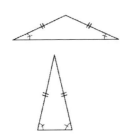

Isosceles Triangle: a type of triangle that has two sides of equal length; also, the angles opposite the equal sides have equal degree measures. Note the two possibilities for an isosceles triangle at the left: two equal short sides and one long side, or two equal long sides and one short side. If it helps, you can remember these possibilities as the "molehill" isosceles (top) and the "mountain" isosceles (bottom).

Equilateral Triangle: a type of triangle composed of three sides of equal length and three vertices measuring 60 degrees each. The triangle at the right is an example of an equilateral triangle.

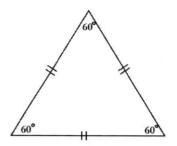

Right Triangle: a type of triangle with two sides that meet at a right (90-degree) angle. The side opposite the right angle is the longest side of the triangle and is called the ***hypotenuse***. The other two sides are often referred to as ***legs***. The triangle at the left is an example of a right triangle.

To Calculate a Triangle's Area: Apply the formula $a = \frac{1}{2} * b * h$, where b is the base of the triangle and h is the height perpendicular to the base. The triangle at the right has these measurements marked. In a right triangle, the height and base are the legs. <u>*Included in Reference Information*</u>

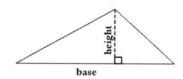

Triangle Inequality: In order for a triangle to exist in the plane, the sum of the lengths of any two of its sides must be greater than the length of the third side.

Another way of looking at it is that in any given triangle, one side's length must be *less than the sum of* and *greater than the difference of* the other two sides. If a problem tells you the lengths of two sides of a triangle, then you can determine the possible lengths of the third side, like this:

> *If a triangle has two sides measuring 4 units and 7 units, then which of the following could not be the length of the third side?*
>
> (A) 4
> (B) 7
> (C) 10
> (D) 12

If the first two sides measure 4 and 7, then the third side would need to be *greater than their difference* (3) and *less than their sum* (11). The only answer choice that meets that requirement is (D) 12.

36. Recognize and work with special right triangles

Within right triangles there are two "special" triangles: the **45-45-90** right triangle and the **30-60-90** right triangle. These triangles are called special because their degree measurements result in side lengths that always have the same easy-to-remember proportions. If you are not already familiar with these two triangles, it is worth your time to study them below until you are confident that you know their ratios offhand. As "special" triangles, they are a favorite of standardized tests everywhere. *Included in Reference Information*

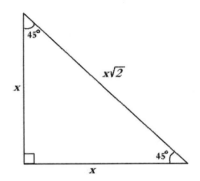
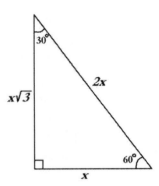

Recognizing these triangles is a quick and trustworthy way to help you fill in diagrams and solve problems without having to go the long way around. Also note that the triangle on the left (the 45-45-90 triangle) is equal to half of a square cut along its ***diagonal***. If you need to measure from one corner of a square to the opposite corner, treat the length like the hypotenuse of a 45-45-90 triangle!

37. Apply the Pythagorean Theorem

For any right triangle, special or otherwise, you can solve for the length of any side as long as you know the lengths of the other two sides by using the ***Pythagorean Theorem***. This theorem states that for any right triangle with legs a and b and hypotenuse c, $a^2 + b^2 = c^2$. Here is an example of the Pythagorean Theorem in action:

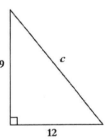

$a^2 + b^2 = c^2$ *Match up the sides given in the diagram.*

$9^2 + 12^2 = c^2$ *Computing the sum on the left will give you the squared value of c.*

$81 + 144 = c^2$ *Now take the square root of both sides to solve for c.*

$\sqrt{225} = 15 = c$ *There you have it!*

Keep in mind that the Pythagorean Theorem can be used to solve for a leg of the triangle just as well as for the hypotenuse. It's a matter of properly filling in the variables you do know and solving the equation for the one you don't. *Included in Reference Information*

38. Measure and evaluate quadrilaterals

A quadrilateral is a four-sided polygon; it is made up of four straight sides and four angles, and the measures of all four angles add up to 360 degrees. When given these polygons, you will usually be asked to find the **perimeter** (the distance around the polygon) or the **area** (the two-dimensional space it contains). Here are the most commonly tested types of quadrilaterals, along with formulas to calculate their perimeters and areas:

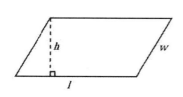

Parallelogram: a quadrilateral composed of two sets of parallel lines. The opposite sides are equal in length, and the opposite angles are equal in degree measure. The perimeter of a parallelogram is equal to twice the sum of the length and width. In other words, $P = 2(l + w)$. To calculate the area of a parallelogram, multiply its length by its height, which must be perpendicular to the length: $A = lh$ (just like a triangle's area must be calculated using base and height). A parallelogram is shown at the left with length l, width w, and height h labeled.

Rectangle: a special case of parallelogram. The opposite sides are equal in length, the opposite angles are equal in degree measure, *and* all angles are right angles (90°). The perimeter of a rectangle can be calculated just like that of a parallelogram: $P = 2(l + w)$. The area of a rectangle can be calculated simply by multiplying the length and width: $A = lw$. A rectangle is shown at the right with length l and width w labeled. *Included in Reference Information*

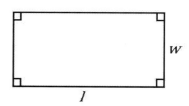

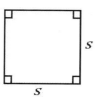

Square: a special case of rectangle. The opposite sides are equal in length, the opposite angles are equal in degree measure, all angles are right angles (90°), *and* all side lengths are equal. A square's perimeter equals the side length times 4 ($P = 4s$), and the area can be calculated by squaring the side length ($A = s^2$). A square is shown at the left with side length s labeled.

39. Measure and evaluate other polygons

Aside from triangles and quadrilaterals, a few other **regular polygons** can show up on the test. A regular polygon is a polygon in which all side lengths are equal and all angle measures are equal; equilateral triangles and squares are regular polygons.

Here are three common regular polygons:

Pentagon (5 sides) *Hexagon (6 sides)* *Octagon (8 sides)*

For any regular polygon, calculate the perimeter by multiplying the side length by the number of sides. Note that these regular polygons can be divided into other shapes that are easier to work with if you need to calculate the area or the length from one **vertex** (corner) to another.

As shown at the right, a regular hexagon can be divided into six equal equilateral triangles.

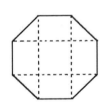

As shown at the left, an octagon can be divided into a square, four 45-45-90 triangles, and four rectangles. (You could also add line segments around it to make a larger square with four 45-45-90 triangles cut out of it.)

For any polygon, regular or not, you can determine the sum of its interior angle measures by using one of two methods.

To find your answer visually, start from one vertex of the polygon and see how many triangles you can make by drawing lines from that vertex to other vertices. Each triangle's interior angles add up to 180, so multiply the number of triangles by 180 to determine the total angle measure. An example is given at the right.

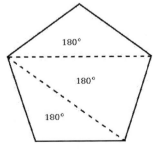

3 triangles * 180° = 540°

If you prefer to stick with a formula, then stick with this one: The sum of degrees inside that polygon equals 180 times the number of sides minus 2. In other words, when n equals the number of sides in the polygon, $sum\ of\ degrees = 180(n-2)$.

If a question gives you complex or irregular shapes and asks you to calculate the area or perimeter, **always look for familiar polygons**. For example, consider this very difficult question:

What is the area of the figure at the right?

(A) $36\sqrt{3}$
(B) $72\sqrt{3}$
(C) $108\sqrt{3}$
(D) $144\sqrt{3}$

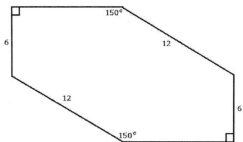

This is one of those frustrating problems that looks like it hasn't given you enough information. The polygon you're given has no regularity to it, and all the answer choices have radicals in them when there aren't even any radicals in the diagram.

Don't panic! Instead, look for a way to start filling in information that you *do* know, whether that's by splitting up the figure into smaller pieces or adding around it to make a familiar shape. For instance:

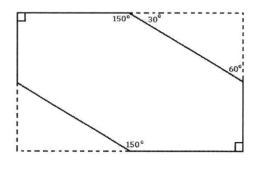

This is much better already, right? By squaring off the corners, you're looking at a rectangle with two 30-60-90 right triangles cut out of it. If you can find the area of the rectangle and subtract the area of the triangles, you'll be all set! Keep filling in information until you have all the measurements you need.

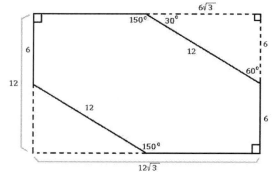

Now you have everything you need: the length and width of the rectangle and the base and height of the triangle (of which there are two). Start calculating and subtracting those areas!

The rectangle's area is its length times its width: $A = 12\sqrt{3} * 12 = 144\sqrt{3}$

Each triangle's area is its base times its height times $\frac{1}{2}$: $A = \frac{1}{2}(6 * 6\sqrt{3}) = 18\sqrt{3}$

The original figure's area is the area of the rectangle minus the area of the two triangles:

$$144\sqrt{3} - 2(18\sqrt{3}) = 144\sqrt{3} - 36\sqrt{3} = 108\sqrt{3}$$

You might have also considered cutting the figure into smaller shapes instead, and that works just as well. Here's what that could look like in this problem:

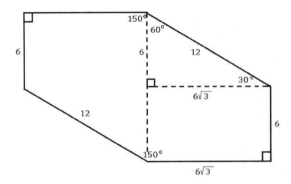

With this method you create two identical smaller rectangles and two identical 30-60-90 triangles. You can therefore find the area of one rectangle and one triangle, add them together, and double the result. It will still come out $108\sqrt{3}$.

40. Measure and evaluate circles

Unlike polygons, which are composed of line segments and vertices, a circle is composed of a single curve around a point called the **center**. Every point on the circle's curve is **equidistant** from the center. Here are the key measurements of circles and formulas to find them:

Radius: the distance from the center to any point on its edge, noted as r in the diagram at the right. The radius is the building block of a circle; you need it to calculate most other measurements pertaining to circles.

Diameter: the distance across a circle through its center, noted as d in the diagram at the right. The diameter is twice the length of the radius. $d = 2r$

Circumference: a circle's perimeter (the distance around its edge), noted as C in the diagram at the right. The circumference is twice the radius times **pi**, an irrational number expressed as π (approximated as 3.14). $C = 2\pi r$. _Included in Reference Information_

Area: the measure of two-dimensional space contained by a circle, usually noted as *A*. The area is **pi** times the radius squared. $A = \pi r^2$. *Included in Reference Information*

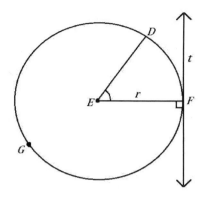

Tangent: a line that runs alongside a circle and intersects it at exactly one point. At the point of intersection, the tangent is perpendicular to the radius. In the diagram at the left, the tangent is labeled with *t*.

Sector: a "wedge" or "pie piece" of a circle, bounded by part of the circumference and two **radii** (the plural of radius). In the diagram at the left, the area contained by points *D*, *E*, and *F* is a sector.

Angle measure: a piece of the a circle's angles around its center. The angles of a circle will always add up to 360°. Sector *DEF* shown in the diagram at the left has an angle measure of approximately 60°.

Arc: a piece of the circle's circumference. **Minor** arcs, like arc *DF* in the diagram at the left, are less than half of the circumference, and **major** arcs, like arc *DGF* in the diagram at the left, are more than half the circumference.

Sector area: the area of a "wedge" or "pie piece" of a circle. The area of a sector can be calculated by finding the circle's total area and multiplying it by quantity of the sector's angle measure divided by 360°. For example, sector *DEF* shown in the diagram at the left has an angle measure of approximately 60°, so to find its area, the circle's total area should be multiplied by $\frac{60°}{360°}$.

It's important to note that these parts of a circle are always in proportion to one another.

$$\frac{angle\ measure}{360°} = \frac{arc\ length}{circumference} = \frac{sector\ area}{total\ area}$$

If a question gives an arc length and asks for the area of a sector, for instance, you can convert quickly from one to the other by setting up a proportion and cross-multiplying.

41. Calculate midpoints, slopes, and distance on the coordinate plane

Geometry concepts can also be presented on the coordinate plane, and there are three main measurements you should know how to make: midpoint, slope, and distance.

Midpoint: the point between two other given points on the coordinate plane, such that it is equidistant from each given point. The way to calculate the midpoint of two given points on the coordinate plane is simply to average their coordinates together. For example, the midpoint of $(-1,4)$ and $(3,6)$ is $(\frac{-1+3}{2}, \frac{4+6}{2})$, or $(1,5)$.

Slope: the change in *y*-values divided by the change in *x*-values in a line on the coordinate plane, also known as "***rise over run***." Slope can be calculated by using any two points on a line. Slope is also discussed in Concept 10: "Analyze a linear function graph." On the coordinate plane, parallel lines have identical slopes, and perpendicular lines have opposite reciprocal slopes. For instance, if you were looking at linear function $f(x) = 2x + 1$, a line parallel to that function would also have a slope of 2, and a line perpendicular to that function would have a slope of $-\frac{1}{2}$.

Distance: the linear measurement between two points on the coordinate plane. Between points (x_1, y_1) and (x_2, y_2), the distance can be calculated with the ***Distance Formula***:
$d = \sqrt{(x_1 - x_2)^2 + (y_1 - y_2)^2}$

Does the Distance Formula look vaguely terrifying? No worries! It's really just the high-maintenance cousin of a much friendlier formula: the Pythagorean Theorem!

If you square both sides of the Distance Formula, it looks like this:

$d^2 = (change\ in\ x\ values)^2 + (change\ in\ y\ values)^2$ ... Or ... $c^2 = a^2 + b^2$

So if you need to find the distance between two points on the coordinate plane, keep in mind that you're basically just solving for the hypotenuse of a right triangle. You can even draw it out that way if it's helpful to you!

42. Use trigonometric ratios

Trigonometry is now included on the SAT for the first time. It is a type of math that focuses upon triangles and how their lengths relate to each other. Specifically, with right triangles the three side lengths and three angle measures relate to one another in specific proportions, and you can use ***trigonometric ratios*** to convert from the angle measure of one vertex to the length of a side (or vice versa).

There are three basic ratios in trigonometry, always pertaining to a specific angle. The angle in question is usually noted with the Greek letter ***theta***, or θ.

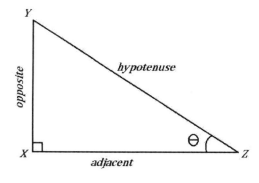

Sine: the ratio of the side opposite angle θ to the hypotenuse. This ratio is written as $\sin \theta = \frac{opposite}{hypotenuse}$. In the figure to the left, the sine of θ is equal to side *XY* divided by side *YZ*.

Cosine: the ratio of the side adjacent angle θ to the hypotenuse. This ratio is written as $\cos \theta = \frac{adjacent}{hypotenuse}$. In the figure to the left, the cosine of θ is equal to side *XZ* divided by side *YZ*.

Tangent: the ratio of the side opposite angle θ to the side adjacent angle θ. This ratio is written as $\tan \theta = \frac{opposite}{adjacent}$. In the figure to the left, the tangent of θ is equal to side *XY* divided by side *XZ*. (

> *(Note that the trigonometric ratio **tangent** is different than a **tangent line** in a question involving circles.)*

The trigonometric ratios can be remembered using the mnemonic device SOHCAHTOA, which stands for the abbreviated versions of the three ratios in order.

$$\sin = \frac{O}{H} \qquad \cos = \frac{A}{H} \qquad \tan = \frac{O}{A}$$

43. Use congruence and similarity theorems

Congruence and similarity are two key terms within geometry. They refer to how shapes relate to one another. Here are quick definitions of both:

Congruence: occurs when two shapes have the exact same angle measures and the exact same side lengths. In other words, the two shapes are identical. This is true even if they are reflected or rotated images of one another, as long as the angles and sides can be matched up correctly.

Similarity: occurs when two shapes have the exact same angle measures but different side lengths. Because the angles are the same, the side lengths will remain in ***proportion*** to one another. This means that, for example, if two right triangles have the same angle measures but the length of the first triangle's hypotenuse is twice that of the second triangle, then the other side lengths of the first triangle will also be twice the length of those of the second triangle.

44. Measure and evaluate three-dimensional/solid figures

One of the toughest geometry skills on a standardized math test is visualizing a three-dimensional shape on a two-dimensional page. Questions like these were more common on previous versions of the SAT, but they are still complicated enough to be worth a careful review. Here are two of the most commonly tested three-dimensional shapes:

The ***right rectangular prism***, or box (left), is composed of three measurements—length, width, and height—that create six ***faces*** and contain a three-dimensional space. A ***cube***, or three-dimensional square, is a type of rectangular prism for which all three of those measurements are equal (just like the side lengths of a square).

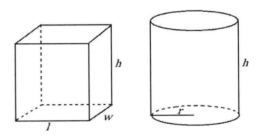

The ***right cylinder*** (right) is composed of two measurements—radius and height—that create two circular ***bases*** and one continuous "wraparound" face and contain a three-dimensional space.

The term ***right*** in these shapes means that their sides are perpendicular to their bases. A three-dimensional shape that is not right is called "skewed," but those types of shapes are not tested.

Other shapes that *could* show up include spheres (three-dimensional circles), pyramids, cones, and prisms with triangular or other polygonal bases. We're not detailing each of those here because they are so rarely tested, but several of them are given in the Reference Information at the start of each Math section.

There are three measurements you should know how to calculate for three-dimensional figures: ***volume***, ***surface area***, and ***distance***. The next three concepts review each of those measurements in turn.

45. Calculate volume

Volume is the amount of three-dimensional space that an object or figure contains. It is calculated in various ways depending on the shape of the figure, but the principle is the same: *For any right prism or cylinder, multiply the area of the base with the height.* The formulas for less commonly tested three-dimensional shapes are trickier to memorize offhand, but *all* of the basic volume formulas are *Included in Reference Information*. Here are the basics of volume:

Rectangular prism: calculated by multiplying the length, width, and height. $V = lwh$

Cylinder: calculated by multiplying the area of the circular base, where r is the radius, and the height. $V = \pi r^2 h$

Sphere: calculated by multiplying the area of the largest circle contained by the sphere (πr^2), where r is the radius, and the quantity $\frac{4}{3} r$. $V = \frac{4}{3} \pi r^3$

Cone: calculated by multiplying the area of the circular base, where r is the radius, by one-third of the height. $V = \frac{1}{3} \pi r^2$

Pyramid: calculated by multiplying the length, width, and height by one-third. $V = \frac{1}{3} lwh$

46. Calculate surface area

Surface area (S.A.) is the ***sum of the areas of all the surfaces*** of a three-dimensional object or figure. One way to picture surface area is to visualize what a shape would look like if it were flattened out, like a cardboard box cut open and stretched out flat. Again, the shapes for which you will need to find surface area are chiefly rectangular prisms and cylinders. Here are methods for finding each:

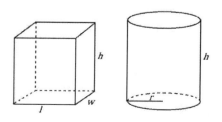

Rectangular prism: Think of its surface area as three pairs of sides—bottom and top (*length times width*), front and back (*length times height*), and left and right (*width times height*). For a rectangular prism, therefore, $S.A. = 2(lw) + 2(lh) + 2(wh)$.

Cylinder: Think of its surface area as two circles and a rectangle that wraps around like a label on a soup can. The bases are πr^2 each, and the area of the rectangle is the ***circumference*** of the base times height. For a cylinder, then, $S.A. = 2(\pi r^2) + 2\pi r h$.

47. Calculate three-dimensional distance

One of the toughest things to do in three-dimensional geometry is to calculate distance because distance is a one-dimensional concept. However, in order to measure distance in a three-dimensional figure, you need to use *two*-dimensional concepts as well! The key to solving for three-dimensional distance is to **work in two dimensions at a time**.

Sound confusing? Don't panic! Here's an example to illustrate how you can do it:

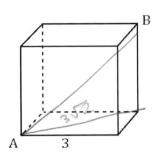

In the cube shown above, what is the distance from point A to point B?

(A) $3\sqrt{2}$
(B) $3\sqrt{3}$
(C) $3\sqrt{6}$
(D) $6\sqrt{6}$

Remember, when you are working with complex geometric diagrams, it is helpful to do two things: **draw in additional information**, and **look for familiar shapes**. Start there.

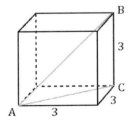

Drawing in a line from point A to point B helps, because you can see that the line travels across three dimensions: *over*, *back*, and *up*.

Since this is a cube, all side lengths are equal, so you can fill in the length of 3 to help you remember.

Adding in a *point C* (across the base from point A and down from point B) is a key step to make this a lot clearer. Point C will allow you to work with two dimensions at a time. Think of it this way:

If you were to look at the cube from above, the base would look like a square, right? And the distance across the base is a **diagonal** of that square. You can use either the Pythagorean Theorem or your knowledge of the 45-45-90 special right triangle to determine the distance from point A to point C: $3\sqrt{2}$.

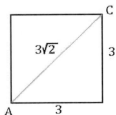

203

Well, $3\sqrt{2}$ is an answer choice. Are we done? *Nope!* We've only measured across the base—over and back—so we still need to measure that third dimension: *up*.

Since the length of AC runs across the two-dimensional base, it is perpendicular to the cube's height just like the rest of the base. That means that the distance from point A to point B is the **hypotenuse** of a right triangle—Triangle ACB—and you now have the measurements of both legs of that triangle. Use the Pythagorean Theorem to solve for the hypotenuse.

$a^2 + b^2 = c^2$

$3^2 + (3\sqrt{2})^2 = c^2$

$9 + 18 = c^2$

$27 = c^2$

$c = \sqrt{27} = 3\sqrt{3}$

$3\sqrt{3}$ is the distance from point A to point B. That's how you measure three-dimensional distance!

48. Work with imaginary numbers

Imaginary numbers? Aren't the real ones bad enough?!

We know. The previous version of the SAT did not include imaginary numbers, but apparently the test makers decided that it was time to make things a little more *eeeevil*. Here are the basics of imaginary numbers:

i is the basis of imaginary numbers—it is defined as the square root of –1, or $\sqrt{-1}$.

All other imaginary numbers are written in terms of *i*; for example, while $\sqrt{9} = 3$, $\sqrt{-9}$ can be expressed as $3i$. If you need to combine a real number and imaginary number—also known as a **complex number**—write the terms in the form $a + bi$, where *a* is the real number and *b* is the coefficient for *i*.

Sometimes *i* will be raised to powers greater than 1. When that happens, remember this pattern:

$i^1 = \sqrt{-1}$

$i^2 = -1$

$i^3 = -i$

$i^4 = 1$

This pattern is infinite, so i^5 will be the same as i^1, i^{12} will be the same as i^4, and so on. If you can memorize that pattern, it will be a valuable tool when a question about imaginary numbers comes up.

49. Convert between degrees and radians

Degrees and radians are simply two units for measuring the circumference of a circle. A circle consists of 360 degrees, or 2π radians, and converting between them is a useful skill, especially when you progress into subjects like trigonometry and pre-calculus.

As mentioned in the geometry review above, circumference (distance around the circle's edge) equals twice the radius times pi, or $C = 2\pi r$. Therefore, the radius reaches around the circle 2π times.

That means that a radian is the length of the radius wrapped around the edge of the circle, and that length is equal to a certain number of degrees out of 360. Follow the rules below to convert between these two measurements.

From radians to degrees
Multiply the number of radians by $\frac{180}{\pi}$.

Example: $4\pi \; radians = 4\pi * \left(\frac{180}{\pi}\right) = 720 \; degrees$

From degrees to radians
Multiply the number of degrees by $\frac{\pi}{180}$.

Example: $540 \; degrees = 540 * \left(\frac{\pi}{180}\right) = 3\pi$

50. Create or use a two-variable equation to evaluate a circle in the coordinate plane

Evaluating circles in the coordinate plane is a new topic for the new SAT Math Test. It is also a more advanced concept, so don't panic if you haven't seen circles on the coordinate plane in math class yet! Two-variable equations can be assembled to work with circles, and they are really no scarier than quadratic equations once you understand what they mean.

Here is the ***standard form equation*** of a circle: $(x - h)^2 + (y - k)^2 = r^2$

"Wait a minute," you might be thinking, "that equation has *five* variables! I thought you said this was a *two*-variable equation!"

Don't worry—the only variables you'll see in an equation are x and y. The other three will be replaced with numbers. Here's what the equation means, really:

$x^2 + y^2 = r^2$ is the most basic circle, also called a ***parent function***. It looks like this:

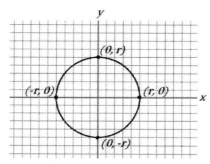

Note that the circle's center is located at the ***origin***, or intersection of the axes: (0,0). The variables x and y make up the circle around it, and r is the radius of the circle. If you refer to the standard form equation above, it's basically the same thing, except that h and k are both equal to 0 in this equation.

What does that mean? It means that when h and k equal anything other than 0 for a circle, they reveal the coordinates of that circle's center: h points to the x-coordinate and k points to the y-coordinate. Look at this circle equation:

$(x - 2)^2 + (y - 4)^2 = 9$

With only that equation to look at, you can determine exactly what this circle looks like on the coordinate plane. The x-coordinate of the center is 2, and the y-coordinate is 4. And if 9 is standing in for r^2, then r must equal 3. Here it is on the coordinate plane:

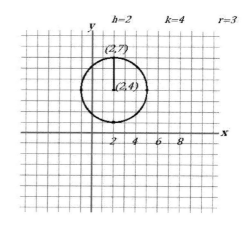

Now let's look at it the other way around. If a question asked you, "What is the equation of a circle with center $(-3, 2)$ and a radius of 5 units?" you could piece that together just as well.

Start with the parent function: $x^2 + y^2 = r^2$

Then fill in what you know. Radius is 5 units? Fill in the radius squared: $x^2 + y^2 = 25$

The center coordinates are $(-3, 2)$, right? Then in the equation they must be $(x + 3)$ and $(y - 2)$.

So what's the equation? $(x + 3)^2 + (y - 2)^2 = 25$.

There, see? No reason to panic. And this is the *last* of the Math Test concepts to review, so give yourself a pat on the back for working through these complex concepts!

Chapter 10: Math Practice Set

On the next several pages are practice problems that resemble the ones you'll see on the Math Test. Whenever you can, practice using the strategies outlined in Chapter 7: Working the Question, Working the Answers, and Working the Test. Good luck!

---

1. Oliver sends t text messages every day. In terms of t, how many text messages will Oliver send in two weeks?
    - (A) $2t$
    - (B) $7t$
    - (C) $10t$
    - (D) $14t$

2. The Allenton Trucking Company needs to deliver 62,000 cubic feet of bedding and pillows to a new Beds & Baths Superstore. Allenton has two truck models: the small trucks can carry loads of 2,400 cubic feet, and the large trucks can carry loads of 4,800 cubic feet. If each truck can only be used for one load, and Allenton has eight small trucks available for the job, how many large trucks will be needed?
    - (A) 7
    - (B) 8
    - (C) 9
    - (D) 10

3. *m* is an even integer, and *n* is an odd integer. Which of the following *must* be even?
   (A) mn
   (B) $m + n$
   (C) n^2
   (D) $m + 1$

4. On a typical fall day, a coffee shop sells *p* pumpkin spice lattes per hour. How many pumpkin spice lattes would the shop sell in one week, if it is open 9am to 9pm each day?
   (A) $12p$
   (B) $84p$
   (C) $120p$
   (D) $168p$

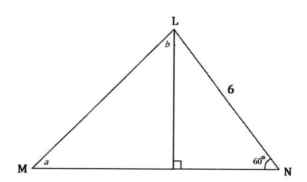

5. Given that angles *a* and *b* are equal in the figure above, what is the length of side **LM**?
   (A) $3\sqrt{2}$
   (B) $3\sqrt{3}$
   (C) $3\sqrt{6}$
   (D) $6\sqrt{3}$

6. If *x* and *y* are both prime numbers, which of the following *cannot* be prime?
   (A) $x + 1$
   (B) $y + 3$
   (C) $2xy$
   (D) $xy + 2$

7. Ellie's Electronics has tablets on sale for *d* dollars each—but wait, there's more! If a customer buys *n* tablets at once, each tablet will cost only *d* – 25 dollars! Which of the following expresses the total cost of purchasing *n* tablets?
   (A) $n(d - 25)$
   (B) $d - 25n$
   (C) $2d - 25$
   (D) $n * d - 25$

8. In an after-school service club, there are four freshmen for every three sophomores, two sophomores for every three juniors, and two juniors for each senior. If there are 9 senior members in the service club, how many freshman members are there?
   (A) 9
   (B) 12
   (C) 16
   (D) 18

9. William has *m* jerseys, *m* + 1 hats, and *m* – 2 pairs of shorts. How many possible combinations of these three articles of clothing (one jersey, one hat, one pair of shorts) can he wear?
   (A) $3m - 1$
   (B) $3m + 1$
   (C) $m^2 - m - 2$
   (D) $m^3 - m^2 - 2m$

10. Kara has invited *f* friends to her movie night, and each friend (plus Kara herself) will eat *p* cups of popcorn. In terms of *f* and *p*, how many cups of popcorn should Kara make in order to have enough for everyone?
    (A) fp
    (B) $fp + 1$
    (C) $p(f + 1)$
    (D) $f(p + 1)$

11. The cost of admission to a theme park is 5 dollars for a child and 10 dollars for an adult. However, with each paid adult admission, one child is admitted for free. Which of the following expresses the cost in dollars of admission for c children and a adults?
    (A) $5(c + 2a - 1)$
    (B) $5c + 10a$
    (C) $5(c - a) + 10a$
    (D) $5(c + a) + 10a$

12. $\sin \frac{\theta}{2}$ equals which of the following?
    (A) $\frac{\pi}{2}$
    (B) π
    (C) $\frac{3\pi}{2}$
    (D) 2π

Questions 13 and 14 are based on the tables below.

Pairs of Shoes Sold at Sal's Shoe Store

	Week 1	Week 2
Sneakers	15	17
Flats	11	9
Heels	18	15
Boots	12	16

Profit Per Pair Sold

	Profit
Sneakers	$20
Flats	$35
Heels	$40
Boots	$35

13. Sal's Shoe Store just opened and is tracking its sales of women's shoes to determine which type is the most profitable. What was Sal's total profit for the four given types of shoes in Week 1?
    (A) $1815.00
    (B) $1825.00
    (C) $1960.00
    (D) $2010.00

14. Which type of shoe produced the greatest profit in Week 2?
    (A) *Sneakers*
    (B) *Flats*
    (C) *Heels*
    (D) *Boots*

15. Jake's apple tree produced g apples in 2003. Between 2003 and 2008, the apple tree's production increased by 25%. Between 2008 and 2013 the tree's production increased by another 20%. What was the total percent increase in production between 2003 and 2013?
    (A) 20%
    (B) 25%
    (C) 45%
    (D) 50%

16. If a cube has a volume of $125m^3$ cubic inches, what is the surface area of the cube in square inches, in terms of m?
    (A) $100m^2$
    (B) $150m^2$
    (C) $300m^2$
    (D) $750m^2$

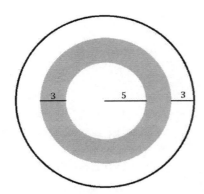

17. A maintenance worker is painting a circular target on the ground for a hot air balloon to land on. The target is shown in the diagram above (all measurements in feet). Given that the target will be painted with a center of white paint, a middle ring of gray paint, and an outer ring of white paint, how many square feet will the gray paint need to cover?
    (A) 25π
    (B) 39π
    (C) 57π
    (D) 64π

18. Sarah is playing a ring toss game with the following rules: each ring that misses the pegs is worth 0 points, each ring that lands on a blue peg is worth 5 points, and each ring that lands on a red peg is worth 10 points. Sarah throws n rings. If half the rings land on blue, $\frac{1}{6}$ land on red, and the rest are misses, how many points does Sarah earn in terms of n?

    (A) $\frac{15}{6}n$
    (B) $10n$
    (C) $\frac{25}{6}n$
    (D) $15n$

19. A farmer sprays a natural-ingredient pesticide over a sample of his soybean plants, to test its effectiveness against the soy beetles attacking his crops. The farmer sprays the pesticide over 100 plants, waits two days, and finds that 92 plants are now beetle-free. Assuming that the pesticide will have the same effectiveness when the farmer sprays his remaining 900 plants, how many of those 900 will still have beetles after two days?

    (A) 72
    (B) 80
    (C) 720
    (D) 828

20. Clark and Gregg have a lawn mowing business. Their best client is Mrs. Applegate, who has the largest lawn in the neighborhood. Clark can mow Mrs. Applegate's lawn in 40 minutes working alone. Gregg can mow the same lawn in 25 minutes working alone. To the nearest minute, how long will it take Clark and Gregg to mow Mrs. Applegate's lawn if they work together?

    (A) 13
    (B) 17
    (C) 21
    (D) 25

Math Practice Set Answers

1. D
2. C
3. A
4. B
5. C
6. C
7. A
8. C
9. D
10. C
11. C
12. D
13. B
14. C
15. D
16. B
17. B
18. C
19. A
20. B

Chapter 11: The Essay Test

Overview

As you can probably guess, the essay portion of the SAT requires you to write an essay. You'll be given a passage to read, a question to answer about the passage, and some space to write an essay that answers that question. In this chapter, we'll cover some of the things you'll need to know before taking the essay portion of the test—or deciding whether to take it at all.

Should I take the essay portion?

Unlike in previous years, the essay portion of the SAT is now optional. Before you decide whether to take the essay portion of the SAT or not, you'll want to consider whether you need it for your college applications. Some colleges and specific programs will require the essay, and some won't. The size of the programs and universities to which you apply and the type of major you plan to pursue (liberal arts versus engineering, for example) could affect whether you'll need the essay.

If you want to apply to a school or a program that doesn't require the SAT essay, you might want to take the essay portion anyway. If your score is good, you can still include it in your application, and both the score itself and the fact that you included it may make you more competitive. Whatever your plans, though, check all requirements carefully, and check them several months before the application deadline. You wouldn't want to be contacted by an admissions office wondering where your essay score is with a tight deadline and no upcoming SAT test dates. When in doubt, keep in mind that it would be better to *have* an essay score and not *need* it than to *need* it and not *have* it.

Let's assume you will be taking the SAT essay test. You probably have some questions at this point, such as…

How does the SAT Essay Test work?

The SAT essay is based on a reading passage. You'll be given a passage that's about 650 to 750 words long, which is usually some kind of persuasive essay or speech about a complex subject. If you don't know anything about the subject of the passage, don't worry—the prompt focuses on how the passage is written, not on what it's about. You just have to work with the passage that's in front of you.

The prompt will ask you to analyze how the author of the passage builds an argument to persuade an audience to see the issue his or her way. (Every essay prompt will ask you to do that, which means we can get a lot more specific in this study guide about how to answer the prompt than we could if every prompt were different.) Whether you agree or disagree with the author doesn't matter, and you won't be asked for your own opinion. You just need to analyze how the author presented his or hers.

Your answer booklet will include roughly two and a half lined pages. You'll have 50 minutes for the essay portion of the test. You don't have to take up all the space or all the time, but you won't get more of either, so plan carefully.

How will the essay be scored?

The SAT essays are scored by live humans who are well-trained in the scoring criteria and procedures. Sure, essays are subjective, but computers can't score them (at least, not yet), and the folks in charge really do train the human graders to be fair, consistent, and accurate.

But what you were probably wondering was what those live human graders are looking for. That's important information, especially when you're trying to figure out what you should put in your essay, right? Right.

Your essay will be scored by two graders, each of whom will score it on a scale of 1 to 4 in each of three categories. Those two scores in each category will be added together, so you'll end up with a score of 2 to 8 in each category.

The three categories in which your essay will be scored are:

Reading: This score measures how well you can understand the text, evaluate its structure and main ideas, and interpret what it's saying. Using a few well chosen quotations and paraphrases will boost your Reading score by demonstrating that you have a good grasp of what the text is saying.

Analysis: This score measures how well you can relate the passage to the prompt, identify and evaluate how the author uses reasoning and evidence, and support your own claims about what the author is saying (like whether an argument is logical or whether a persuasive technique is effective). Make sure that you not only cite *what* evidence and arguments the author uses, but also explain *how* the author uses those things to persuade his or her audience.

Writing: This score measures how well you organize and write your essay. It includes things like your thesis, the flow of your argument, your transitions between paragraphs and ideas, and your use of appropriate style, tone, and word choice. It also includes things like grammar, spelling, and punctuation. If the Reading and Analysis scores focus on how well you can answer the prompt, the Writing score focuses on how well you can actually, you know, write.

Cecil's Tips to Stay Sharp

Don't worry what would happen if one grader gave your essay a 4 and the other gave it a 1. That kind of thing is really rare, but if it happens the College Board has a procedure for making sure your essay ends up with the correct score.

It's important to note that these three categories are scored across your whole essay. In other words, when you're actually writing, you won't break your essay down into separate sections where you're trying to deal with Reading, Analysis, and Writing in turn. One of the things the graders will look for is how well your essay flows—smooth, logical transitions will get you a higher score than choppy, disjointed ones—so treat your essay as a whole essay rather than as three separate categories of stuff crammed together.

How do I start my essay once the test begins?

The first thing you'll want to do is skip over the passage and read the prompt. Make sure you know what you'll be asked to write about, so you have a good idea of what to look for as you read. Pay attention to the wording of the prompt, because that can affect what you look for in the passage and how you write your essay.

Then read the passage. But don't just sit there and let it float past your eyes—read actively! Underline things, circle things, draw arrows linking things to other things, write notes in the margins, whatever will help you get a better grip on what the passage says and how the passage says it. Remember that active reading strategy discussed back in Chapter 2? Do that. Actively read the heck out of that passage.

Next, take a few minutes to plan your essay. Find some empty space in the margins of the essay page of your test booklet, and jot down a brief, informal outline—just enough to keep yourself on track and to keep your thoughts in a logical order. Note what you want your thesis to be, which arguments and pieces of evidence you want to cite, what you want to say about each one, and how you want to wrap up. A few key words for each of those things will probably do the trick.

Then start writing. Refer to your outline, the passage, and the prompt frequently. Use paragraphs to keep your ideas organized, and use clear, precise words and sentences to express those ideas. Give your essay a solid introduction with a clear thesis, and wrap it up with a strong, tidy conclusion.

Leave a few minutes for proofreading. Go back over your essay, fix any mistakes you might find, and revise anything that needs revising. Look for any issues with *how* you wrote (things like your grammar, spelling, punctuation, tone, word choice, clarity, and organization) and *what* you wrote (things like your thesis, examples, explanations and reasoning, and focus). Maybe you'll find some things to fix and you'll be glad you left yourself time to do it, or maybe you'll find that your essay is in good shape and you'll be glad for the extra boost of confidence. Either way, proofreading will be well worth those few minutes!

How should I organize my essay?

There aren't any hard-and-fast rules for how to organize your SAT essay. You do need to make sure that your essay is clear and easy to follow, however, so that means you should come up with an organizational plan that makes sense and then stick with that plan for your entire essay.

The next four paragraphs outline one organizational strategy you may find useful. We think it's pretty solid, but if you think a different one would serve you better, go for it. Just remember that, no matter how you organize your essay, it needs to be clear and easy to follow. You'll want some kind of introduction and conclusion, a logical progression of ideas, and smooth transitions from one major idea to the next.

One possible organizational strategy

Start with an introduction paragraph, no more than three or four sentences long. Your main goal here is to draw the readers in and give them a sense of what you're about to write and why they should pay attention. One good strategy is to start by describing a relevant real-life situation your readers will probably recognize; another is to start by describing the context for the passage, which is usually briefly stated at the beginning. Lay out the context of your essay for your readers—what the central issue is, what passage you're responding to, what the passage's author argues, that sort of thing. At or near the end of that paragraph, you should state your thesis; more on that below.

Then you'll get into the body of your paper. You should divide this part of your essay into paragraphs of a few sentences each, with a new paragraph for each major idea and good transitions between paragraphs. This is where you'll unpack the reasons behind the opinion you state in your thesis. Cite evidence from the passage, and then—this is important—explain how that evidence supports your thesis.

You should try to cite three or four different arguments or pieces of evidence in this part of your paper. The author might use more than three or four, but don't worry about finding all of them; just pick the ones you think are especially important, and talk about those. It's also worth noting that the graders aren't looking for you to give the "right" answer or cite the "right" pieces of evidence. They're looking for you to present good, clear explanations for whichever pieces you do cite. In other words, your "whys" are more important than your "whats."

Finally, wrap up your essay with a conclusion paragraph that makes your readers feel as though you have actually finished your essay and not just stopped writing. One good way to conclude your essay is with a restatement of your thesis and a brief summary of your evidence. An even better way is to follow the summary of your thesis and evidence with a little additional analysis of the passage as a whole. For example, if you weren't convinced by the author's argument, what might have convinced you? If you were convinced, what did you think was the author's strongest point? Whether you thought the author's argument was effective or not, what might he or she have done to make it stronger? Try answering one of those questions, or a similar one of your own, to finish strong.

An organizational pitfall to watch out for

Some schools teach students to structure an essay in very particular ways. For example, one commonly taught strategy says that in the introduction you should tell the reader what you're going to tell them, then in the body you should actually tell them, then in the conclusion you should tell them what you've just told them. What the teachers don't mention is that this scheme can get dreadfully repetitive and boring unless you're *really* careful with it. It's also a poor use of the limited space you have for your SAT essay. Why waste space saying the same thing three times when there are so many more great ideas and arguments you can discuss instead?

Now, in the organizational strategy we outlined above, we did suggest a three-part structure kind of like the ones we're arguing against here, so maybe it seems like we're giving you mixed messages. But don't just *use* the basic three-part structure; *build* on it.

Notice that we suggested that the introduction include some context for the passage and that the conclusion include some brief additional analysis, elements which are not repeated elsewhere in the essay. And remember that you're already giving your readers your whole argument in the body of your essay, so you don't need to preview too much of it in the introduction or recap it in detail in the conclusion. At most, you just want to allude to your evidence in a few words in your conclusion to jog your readers' memory a little. Following these suggestions will make your essay more interesting and less repetitive.

If you want to use an essay structure that you've learned in school, go ahead; if you want to use a different one, that's up to you. Your English teacher will never see your SAT Essay, after all. Just make sure that whatever structure you use is clear and easy for the graders to follow.

How do I generate a thesis statement?

Your essay should have a thesis statement, one that clearly and directly addresses the prompt; the graders will be looking for it. Since the prompt will ask you to analyze how the author of the passage constructed his or her argument to persuade the intended audience, your thesis should deal with what evidence, arguments, and techniques the author used or—better still—with how effective you think the author's arguments were.

Try asking yourself a question, such as "Does the author make a strong, successful case for his or her opinion or not?" or "Is the author's argument effective, ineffective, or a little of both?" Your answer to that question can be your thesis, and the reasons for your answer should be the evidence you present to support your thesis.

One strong place to put your thesis statement is at the end of your first paragraph. Use the first few sentences of that paragraph to introduce your essay by setting up the context for the passage, the major issue at hand, and the point the speaker was trying to argue. Then state your thesis clearly and directly. Then, in a new paragraph, begin presenting the evidence to support your thesis, which will make up the body of your essay.

Remember that your opinion on the issue discussed in the passage is irrelevant and should *not* be your thesis. You're being asked how the author constructed an argument about that issue, so focus your thesis on that question. See the section on page 230 about "The Soapbox Essay" for more about keeping your own opinion from dominating your essay.

How do I analyze the passage?

To analyze something means to break it down into simple parts and examine the parts. That's what you're being asked to do with the passage in your SAT essay—to examine some of the parts of the passage and explain how the author uses those parts to persuade his or her audience.

What the parts are and how they'll get used depends on the passage, of course. An author might try to build a logical case for the correctness of an idea, spur the audience to action by swaying their emotions, or use a different strategy. A passage might include personal anecdotes, references to works of literature or art, statistics, logical reasoning, or any number of other elements and techniques—and probably more than one kind.

As you read the passage, first try to identify the author's opinion on the issue. (The prompt may even do this part for you.) What is the main thing he or she wants the audience to understand? How does he or she want them to think differently about that issue? What does the author want the audience to do differently after reading the passage? Should they vote a certain way, donate money to a certain cause, live their daily lives differently, or what?

Make sure to read the passage actively. Mark where the author presents a new reason, a new statistic, a new anecdote, and so on. Mark where the author seems to be stirring the audience's emotions in one direction or another. Mark where the author seems to be trying to unite people in pursuit of his or her goal—or divide them and pit them against one another. What you'll find in the passage will depend upon the passage itself, but these are general suggestions of common key elements to look for.

As we noted earlier, you'll want to identify several arguments, appeals, techniques, or pieces of evidence that you think are the most important so you can focus your essay on those. And limit the arguments you select to three or four.

Cecil's Tips to Stay Sharp

Don't worry about trying to guess which arguments the graders might think are most important. How well you analyze the arguments that you choose matters far more than which ones you choose.

You'll need more than one or two arguments to demonstrate your analytical skills well, but an essay that gives good, thorough analysis of a few arguments will also score higher than one that identifies every argument in the passage but doesn't leave room to analyze them.

For each of the key elements you select, explain how it helps the author persuade his or her audience. Why does the author include it? How is it meant to work upon the minds or hearts of the audience to move them to the author's point of view? If you think the evidence is effective, why do you think so? If not, why not—and why do you think the author included it anyway?

You don't have to answer each of those questions, but they're worth keeping in mind, because that's the kind of analysis the graders will be looking for, and those questions will help you take your analysis to a good depth. For each piece of evidence, make sure you identify the element you're going to talk about (an easy step to overlook if you're focused on your analysis), then explain how the author uses it, and then give your analysis.

What if I hate the passage or don't understand it?

Rest assured, you can write a good essay on a passage even if you don't like the passage very much. Just draw up your outline, write your essay, and proofread, like you would with any other essay, and after the 50 minutes are up you'll be done with it and you can move on. You can even argue in your essay that the author of the passage didn't make a very convincing case for whatever his or her opinion was.

The question of not understanding the passage is more important, but there is an answer. Remember learning about active reading in Chapter 2? Hopefully, you read the passage actively and marked it up the first time through. If you did all that and you still don't really know what the author was saying, don't panic. You have 50 minutes for this part of the test. Just take a deep breath and read the passage again—and if you didn't read the passage actively the first time, read it actively now!

What kind of tone should I set in my essay?

The tone, mood, and voice of any piece of writing help build the relationship between the author and the readers. When you're trying to decide what tone, mood, and voice to adopt, you should think about who your audience will be and what you want them to know, feel, or understand after they've read your essay.

For the SAT Essay Test, your audience is the graders: neutral, intelligent adults. You want to persuade them that your analysis of the passage is sound and your conclusions are logical. Thus, a calm, rational tone will serve you better than a fiery, impassioned tone. To get a high score, you'll have to emphasize your logical and analytical skills.

How intelligent are the graders? Well, each has at minimum a college degree, so they don't need you to tell them who George Washington was or what two plus two is. You'll want to avoid slang and excessively casual ways of writing, but you don't need to impress the graders with big words or stiffly formal grammar, either. Stick with words you're comfortable using and grammar that helps you get your point across clearly and directly.

It may help to imagine that you're writing to a favorite teacher, a parent or older relative, a clergyperson, or some other adult you know and respect. That person likes you, and you can feel comfortable speaking with him or her in your own natural voice, even if you might not talk in quite the same way you would among your friends. Write your essay as though you were addressing that person, and you should hit the right tone pretty easily.

How long should my essay be?

The short answer is: long enough to answer the prompt well. The SAT essay doesn't have a length requirement. The graders won't be looking for you to fill a certain number of lines or use a certain number of words, and they're not going to dock you any points just for writing a short essay.

What they'll dock you points for is writing an essay that's not long enough to answer the question fully. Maybe you gave a pretty good partial answer, but you could have strengthened your essay by including more examples or more analysis of the passage. Maybe your answer was accurate but vague, and you could have strengthened it by including some specific, concrete details. The short truth is that brief essays tend to fall short in analysis and details, so they tend to earn lower scores. You're not getting points for efficient use of space.

Speaking of which…

Will my handwriting cause problems with my essay?

The people who score handwritten essays are trained not to take handwriting into account. Most of them get pretty good at reading a variety of handwriting, too—even the kind of barely-decipherable chicken-scratch that foretells a promising career in medicine.

Cecil's Tips to Stay Sharp

Don't skip lines or leave wide margins other than indents for paragraphs. If you leave an inch or more on either or both sides, then you're sacrificing valuable space!

At the same time, it *is* possible for exceptionally bad handwriting—or exceptionally tiny handwriting, which challenges the resolution limits of the scanners that digitize the essays—to be deemed illegible, in which case you won't get a very high score. This is rare, but it's not unheard of, so take heed.

What happens much more often is that a student's handwriting, although legible, requires more effort than it should to decipher. Some styles of handwriting create the same problem even when they're done neatly. Large, loopy styles can be just as hard to read as scrawly, scratchy ones. If your letters look like huge loops or humps or swirls, then this applies to you, just as much as it applies if your letters look like they were scratched out by a shivering chicken. Very large handwriting can also take up too much space on the page, preventing you from giving a full answer to the prompt. If this sounds like you, then practice writing smaller so you can fit a good, solid essay in the allotted two and a half pages.

If you're not sure whether your handwriting is legible enough, try copying out the following sentences and asking a teacher or friend to read them aloud:

A large fawn jumped quickly over white zinc boxes.

How can razorback-jumping frogs level six piqued gymnasts?

A cozy lummox gave a pen to a smart squid who asked for a job.

If the reader stumbles, you may want to brush up on your handwriting before the test.[1]

Finally, if you have to erase, and especially if you have to erase more than a few words here or there, erase neatly and as thoroughly as you can. The scorers see scans of your essay, not your actual answer booklet, and things that aren't erased well can make the scans very, very difficult to read.

---

1   You may have noticed that these sentences are *pangrams*, sentences that use every letter of the alphabet at least once. Why didn't we use the best-known pangram, "The quick brown fox jumps over the lazy dog?" Because it's so well known that your reader might recognize and recite it instead of reading it, which wouldn't be a very helpful test of your handwriting.

How should I proofread?

Even the best writers need to proofread their work. After you've read the passage and prepared your outline, don't spend the entire rest of your 50 minutes writing the essay. Leave at least a few minutes at the end to go back over what you've written, so you can fix or revise anything that needs fixing or revising.

If you need to insert a word, you can write it above where you want it and use a caret (^) to refer to it. If you need to add a sentence or phrase, then you can write it after the end of your essay and place an asterisk (*) wherever you want to add it in.

When you proofread your essay (and notice that we said "when," not "if"), you're looking for potential problems in two major categories. One category is the mechanics of writing. You can think of the mechanics of writing as the *form* of your essay, if you want. This category includes things like:

- grammar, spelling, and punctuation
- words you inadvertently skipped
- phrases that can be clearer
- transitions that can be stronger or flow better
- slang that should be eliminated
- places you've made your readers guess what you mean instead of telling them explicitly
- tone that wavers in its consistency or appropriateness for a formal essay

The other major category is the content of your answer to the prompt. If the mechanics of writing is the form of your essay, the content of your answer is its *substance*. This category includes things like:

- a clear, strong thesis
- multiple specific, relevant examples supporting that thesis
- clear explanations of how each example supports that thesis
- whether your essay answers the prompt through detailed analysis of the passage
- whether your essay remains focused on the prompt and the passage

You probably won't have time or space to change much of your essay, but any improvements you make will still help your score. The key is to prioritize. What you *don't* want to do is just move through the essay from beginning to end, fixing each problem as you see it. It's hard to spot problems of overall tone or organization that way. Instead, start by quickly re-reading the whole essay so you can get an idea of any problems it has and where they are. Then identify any severe or repeated problems and fix those first if you can; you'll improve your score the most that way.

Once you think you're finished proofreading your essay, if you still have a minute or two, give it the once-over again, just to be sure.

Common Essay Problems (and How to Avoid Them)

Having graded hundreds of students' essays and written (what feels like) hundreds of our own, we've seen certain mistakes crop up again and again. That works to your advantage, because now we can help you avoid making those same mistakes yourself—and avoiding those mistakes will help you to receive a good score on your essay. It will also help you to become a stronger writer in general.

Grammar usage, punctuation, and spelling errors are common (and you can review many of these concepts in Chapter 5), but the most severe problems in student essays are often problems of topic, problems of thesis and evidence, or problems of tone. The cleanest grammar in the world won't help you much if your essay is bogged down with issues like these. In this section, we'll deal with each of these three categories in turn, and we'll discuss a few variations on each kind of problem.

Problems of Topic

For the SAT Essay Test, you'll be expected to maintain focus on the passage and the prompt all the way through your essay. If you don't do these things, you've got a problem of topic, and there are a few different kinds of those.

> ***The Just Plain Off-Topic Essay:*** The Just Plain Off-Topic Essay doesn't come anywhere near the prompt or passage. Maybe the passage is boring, or you don't understand it, or you just don't feel up to writing a serious essay that day. But you've got fifty minutes to kill and two and a half blank pages to fill, so you start writing. Something. Anything. A poem, a stream-of-consciousness diatribe, a

short story. Props for creativity, but that's not how the SAT essay works. If the passage is about the importance of vocational training in schools, but you write an action-packed story about kung-fu dinosaurs from Jupiter, you won't get a good score.

How to Avoid the Just Plain Off-Topic Essay: Read the passage and the prompt you're given. If you didn't understand the passage or thought it was boring, review page 224 for a section that specifically discusses what to do in that situation. Once you've read and understood the passage, ask yourself, "What is my answer to this prompt, based on this passage?" Then spend a few minutes jotting down an outline that identifies what your answer is and why, based on evidence in the passage, you think it's a good answer. Then write that essay. The whole time, keep checking with yourself to make sure your focus is still on the passage and the prompt you're given. Once you're finished writing, review your essay to make sure you haven't gone off the rails somewhere.

The Tangential Essay: The Tangential Essay starts out related to the passage but then goes somewhere else that the prompt never asked it to go. This is a sneaky problem, because each new idea you bring up usually *does* have a logical connection to the one before it. That's not a bad thing, because it helps your essay flow smoothly. But in order for your essay to get a good score, each idea you bring up *also* has to have a logical connection to the passage and the prompt, and if it doesn't, you have a problem.

Maybe you're given a passage about how we need to reduce pollution, and the author says that one reason we need to reduce pollution is that the greenhouse effect is melting the polar ice caps, which in turn means polar bears are running out of places to live. So you start your essay by identifying the author's anti-pollution stance (great!) and citing her argument about how pollution is causing the ice caps to melt (great!), which is destroying the polar bears' habitat (great!), and so the polar bears are encroaching on human towns near the Arctic Circle (grea—wait, did the author mention that?), and one time your family was camping and a black bear came to your campsite and broke into your cooler and ate all your food (OK, you're definitely drifting here), so in conclusion it's important not to leave food lying around one's campsite (true, but not even a tiny bit relevant). Your essay started off well, and you'll get some points for that, but then it lost focus, and that'll hurt you.

How to Avoid the Tangential Essay: Planning ahead is key here. Your outline is your best friend. Make sure you list in your outline all the examples you want to use in your essay. For each example, ask yourself, "How does *this* example help answer the prompt?"—and then jot down your answer in your outline and use it in your essay. If you can't come up with a good answer, ditch that example and think of another one instead. When you write your essay, refer to your outline often, and stick close to the examples, reasons, and other elements you've noted in your outline. Review your essay once you're done, to make sure the essay stays on track and doesn't lose focus somewhere along the way.

The Soapbox Essay: The Soapbox Essay launches into a sermon based on the subject matter of the passage instead of answering the prompt. This is an especially dangerous problem for you if the passage deals with a topic on which you have a strong opinion. Having strong opinions about important issues is great, and arguing for your opinions is a wonderful intellectual exercise—but not here. You're not being asked to present or defend *your* opinion in the SAT essay; you're only being asked to analyze how the author of the passage supports *his or her* opinion. An essay that focuses on the issue instead of on the passage will not get a high score.

How to Avoid the Soapbox Essay: Read the prompt first and keep it in mind while you read the passage. Read the prompt again after you read the passage. Resist the temptation to jump straight into writing your essay; instead, jot down your outline. Make sure you know how everything in your outline contributes to your answer to the prompt. Remind yourself to focus on the passage, not on the issue. Read the prompt again, *then* start writing your essay. Any time you feel your blood boiling, take a deep breath and look back at your outline and the prompt. When you finish your essay, review it, and make sure it stays on track and answers the prompt. If you absolutely can't resist weighing in on the author's point of view, do it by showing how the passage strengthens or undermines itself from the inside rather than bringing in external arguments of your own to attack or defend it. In other words, keep the focus on the passage, not on the issue.

Problems of Thesis and Evidence

In your essay you should not only cite the evidence but also explain how each piece of evidence supports your thesis (remember, you need one). If you don't do these things, you've got a problem of thesis or evidence, and there are a few different kinds of those.

The Thesis without Evidence Essay: The Thesis Without Evidence Essay is full of general terms about the topic of the passage, but it doesn't back itself up with the kinds of specific, concrete details that make for a strong essay. This kind of essay will often be abstract and vague. Remember that one of the major things the graders are looking for is your ability to analyze how the author uses evidence, argument, persuasive techniques, and other elements to persuade his or her audience, and an important part of showing that you can analyze the passage is citing relevant, specific, concrete details that come straight from the passage.

How to Avoid the Thesis without Evidence Essay: When you read the passage, read actively! Underline or circle important parts. Make notes in the margins. In your outline, list the three or four strongest arguments of pieces of evidence the author uses, and include the statistics, anecdotes, or other elements the author cites, along with a brief explanation of how each one supports the author's main point. Review your essay when you're done, and make sure it's loaded with specific details. Ask yourself, "Would someone be able to get the gist of the original passage just from reading my essay?" If not, you might need more evidence from the passage.

The Evidence without a Thesis Essay: The Evidence Without a Thesis Essay may have some kind of introduction describing the passage, or it may just launch straight into presenting and analyzing the evidence. The beginning of the essay ends up feeling unpleasantly abrupt, and the reader is left with little sense of where your essay is headed, what you're actually trying to say, or why all the evidence you're analyzing should matter.

How to Avoid the Evidence without a Thesis Essay: Include a thesis. Once you've read the prompt and the passage, start your outline with a rough thesis. If you're not sure how to write a thesis statement, see the section beginning on page 222 about how to write a thesis statement. As you build your outline, make sure you can explain how each piece of evidence you cite supports your thesis. When you write your essay, make sure you state your thesis clearly—preferably in the first paragraph. As you review your essay, make sure that you've clearly explained how your evidence supports your thesis.

The Evidence that Contradicts the Thesis Essay: The Evidence that Contradicts the Thesis Essay is usually a sign that you just launched right into writing your essay without taking some time to plan it first. It happens when you start making a point that totally disagrees with what you wrote in your first paragraph. It's a problem because one of the things the graders will look for is how you use evidence from the passage to *support* your thesis about the author's argument; if you cite evidence that *undermines* your thesis instead, the answer to how you use your evidence will be "badly" and your score will be "not so great."

When done properly, citing some evidence that appears to counter your thesis *can* work in your favor by showing that you see strengths as well as weaknesses in the passage. In order for this strategy to work, however, the bulk of the evidence you cite will have to support your thesis, and you will also have to explain why you think your thesis is still right in spite of the evidence that seems to contradict it.

How to Avoid The Evidence that Contradicts the Thesis Essay: Plan ahead. As you're making your outline, when you list each piece of evidence you want to cite, ask yourself, "How does this piece of evidence support my thesis?" If you don't have a good answer, drop that piece of evidence and find a different one. If you want to show that the passage has both strengths and weaknesses, that's all right; just make sure most of the evidence you cite does support your thesis, and make sure you explain why the counter-evidence doesn't mean your thesis is wrong.

Problems of Tone

Remember, the tone of your essay should be appropriate to a reasoned discussion of ideas, and it should remain consistent throughout your essay. Problems of tone can take a few different forms.

The Inappropriately Casual Essay: If you find yourself writing your essay in the same tone of voice you use when you're talking with your friends, your tone is probably too casual. Too casual a tone tells the graders that you aren't taking the essay seriously, which means that they might overlook your argument. The slang, figures of speech, and pop culture references or quotes that are perfectly clear to you and your friends may not be clear to the graders. The same principle applies to abbreviations, including common ones like "IDK" or "LOL." Don't make the graders decode what you write; just use words. (Abbreviations and acronyms found in the passage are fine, though, since the graders will have read the passage.)

How to Avoid the Inappropriately Casual Essay: Taking a few minutes to write down an outline before you start writing can help you get into the right frame of mind. When you start writing, remember that you're not talking to your friends and classmates; you're addressing adults who want you to show them how intelligent you are. When you've finished writing, review your essay, and make sure that your words and sentences are clear and that your tone takes the subject of the essay seriously.

The Inappropriately Formal Essay: Being too formal can be just as problematic as being too casual. If you find yourself writing your essay in the tone of voice of a prim and proper schoolmarm—or a student who's terrified of one—your tone is probably too formal. Too formal a tone can sound insincere and may suggest to the graders that you're trying too hard to impress them. Sounding insincere may not *hurt* your score, but it certainly won't *help*, so it's still worth avoiding.

For example, you might use bigger words than you actually need in the hopes that big words will make you sound intelligent. But this strategy can backfire, because not only will you sound insincere, but you'll also risk using a word incorrectly, especially if it's one you're not familiar with. Some of the constructions and phrasings people adopt when they're trying to write formally can also end up sounding stiff and awkward, like when someone turns "a situation I will not put up with" into "a situation with which I will not put up." You can feel your spine stiffen just reading that phrase, no? So can the graders. Again, anything spine-stiffening may or may not *hurt* your score, but it definitely won't *help*.

How to Avoid the Inappropriately Formal Essay: Planning your essay with a good outline and referring to that outline often when you write can help keep your focus on what you're saying rather than on how you're saying it. If you're tempted to use a fancy-sounding word but you aren't absolutely certain what it means, don't use it. And don't be so paranoid about grammar that you stiffen up your writing style; just focus on your meaning. When you're finished writing, review your paper and make sure it sounds clear, sincere, and natural.

The Tone-Shifting Essay: Sometimes an essay begins in one tone and then shifts to another. Maybe it starts out formal and becomes more casual, for instance, or maybe it starts out coolly rational and becomes more impassioned. Tone shifts like these may happen by deliberate choice, but more often they are unconscious. Tone can change gradually if your main elements slowly alter your writing, or it can change abruptly because something breaks your concentration in the middle of the essay, and when you resume writing you're in a different frame of mind. Whatever the case, the graders are looking for a consistent tone, so tone shifts like these can hurt you.

How to Avoid the Tone-Shifting Essay: When you're planning your essay, decide what tone you want to adopt. When you write, keep in mind that the essay is an intellectual exercise, so even if you inject some emotional fire into your writing, you want to make sure that what you're really showing off is your rational and analytical abilities. Pausing briefly before each new paragraph to re-read the previous one may help keep you from veering off into a new tone, especially if something disrupted your concentration in the meantime. When you review your essay, make a mental note of the tone of each paragraph and revise if you find that the tone changes at any point.

Problems and Pitfalls: Summing Up

Don't be frightened by the list of problems and pitfalls we've just given you. We may have taken a few pages to discuss them, but they all boil down to problems of topic, problems of thesis and evidence, and problems of tone. Better still, you can avoid *all* of them by remembering these four simple tips:

- Read the passage and the prompt carefully and stick to them in your essay.

- Make an outline before you begin writing.

- Keep your tone consistent, rational, and appropriate for an adult you like and respect.

- Review your essay after you've finished writing it.

That's not so scary, is it?

Chapter 12: Essay Practice Prompts

Reading about the SAT Essay Test is all well and good, but there's no substitute for practice. We think the most effective way to prepare for the Essay Test is to simulate the conditions of the test as closely as you can so you'll get a good feel not only for what kind of essay you'll be asked to write but also for how much time and space you'll have.

Here are three sample passages you can use for practice (all from public-domain sources). Each passage is accompanied by instructions and a prompt that are similar to the wording you'll see on the actual test. For each passage and prompt below, give yourself two and a half pages of wide-ruled notebook paper or two pages of college-ruled paper (not both sides). That's about how much space you'll have on the Essay Test. You'll be writing your essay on the test by hand, so you should write your practice essays by hand as well.

Set a timer (microwave, cell phone, etc.) for 50 minutes. Don't start reading the passage until you've started the timer, since you won't be able to start reading the passage on the test until the 50 minutes begins. When the timer stops, stop writing and see how far you've gotten; if you finish early (including proofreading), see how much time you have left. Let that help you figure out how to pace yourself on the test.

Don't worry if you run way over or way under the space or time you're allowed. You're just practicing. Your goal here is to practice so you'll feel comfortable with the structure and time restrictions on test day. It will help you learn to pace yourself and lay out your argument over the space you're given.

The first passage starts on the next page. Good luck!

Practice SAT Essay Passage #1

To gain support for the ratification of the Constitution, James Madison, Alexander Hamilton, and John Jay published a series of pamphlets known as The Federalist Papers, *all written under the pseudonym "Publius." This excerpt is from* Federalist #10: The Union as a Safeguard Against Domestic Factions and Insurrection, *believed to be written by James Madison, in which Madison argues that a representative government such as the one proposed in the Constitution will be more effective than a pure democracy at limiting the ability of factions to divide the new nation.*

As you read, consider how Madison uses:
- *evidence, such as facts or examples, to support claims,*
- *reasoning to develop ideas and to connect claims and evidence, and/or*
- *stylistic or persuasive elements, such as word choice or appeals to emotion, to add power to the ideas expressed.*

The apportionment of taxes on the various descriptions of property is an act which seems to require the most exact impartiality; yet there is, perhaps, no legislative act in which greater opportunity and temptation are given to a predominant party to trample on the rules of justice. Every shilling with which they overburden the inferior number, is a shilling saved to their own pockets.

It is in vain to say that enlightened statesmen will be able to adjust these clashing interests, and render them all subservient to the public good. Enlightened statesmen will not always be at the helm. Nor, in many cases, can such an adjustment be made at all without taking into view indirect and remote considerations, which will rarely prevail over the immediate interest which one party may find in disregarding the rights of another or the good of the whole.

The inference to which we are brought is, that the CAUSES of faction cannot be removed, and that relief is only to be sought in the means of controlling its EFFECTS.

If a faction consists of less than a majority, relief is supplied by the republican principle, which enables the majority to defeat its sinister views by regular vote. It may clog the administration, it may convulse the society; but it will be unable to execute and mask its violence under the forms of the Constitution. When a majority is included in a faction, the form of popular government, on the other hand, enables it to sacrifice to its ruling passion or interest both the public good and the rights of other citizens. To secure the public good and private rights against the danger of such a faction, and at the same time to preserve the spirit and the form of popular government, is then the great object to which our inquiries are directed. Let me add that it is the great desideratum by which this form of government can be rescued from the opprobrium under which it has so long labored, and be recommended to the esteem and adoption of mankind.

By what means is this object attainable? Evidently by one of two only. Either the existence of the same passion or interest in a majority at the same time must be prevented, or the majority, having such coexistent passion or interest, must be rendered, by their number and local situation, unable to concert and carry into effect schemes of oppression. If the impulse and the opportunity be suffered to coincide, we well know that neither moral nor religious motives can be relied on as an adequate control. They are not found to be such on the injustice and violence of individuals, and lose their efficacy in proportion to the number combined together, that is, in proportion as their efficacy becomes needful.

From this view of the subject it may be concluded that a pure democracy, by which I mean a society consisting of a small number of citizens, who assemble and administer the government in person, can admit of no cure for the mischiefs of faction. A common passion or interest will, in almost every case, be felt by a majority of the whole; a communication and concert result from the form of government itself; and there is nothing to check the inducements to sacrifice the weaker party or an obnoxious individual. Hence it is that such democracies have ever been spectacles of turbulence and contention; have ever been found incompatible with personal security or the rights of property; and have in general been as short in their lives as they have been violent in their deaths. Theoretic politicians, who have patronized this species of government, have erroneously supposed that by reducing mankind to a perfect equality in their political rights, they would, at the same time, be perfectly equalized and assimilated in their possessions, their opinions, and their passions.

A republic, by which I mean a government in which the scheme of representation takes place, opens a different prospect, and promises the cure for which we are seeking.

Write an essay in which you explain how James Madison builds an argument to persuade his readers that representative government is the most effective way to limit the divisive power of factions. In your essay, analyze how Madison uses one or more of the features listed above the essay (or features of your own choice) to strengthen the logic and persuasiveness of his argument. Be sure that your analysis focuses on the most relevant features of the passage.

Your essay should not explain whether or not you agree with Madison's argument, but rather explain how Madison builds an argument to persuade his readers.

Practice SAT Essay Passage #2

Deaf and blind since early childhood, American author and activist Helen Keller learned to communicate thanks to patient teachers and her own belief that she could succeed. In this excerpt from her essay "Optimism," Keller argues that, in the present as well as in American history, an optimistic outlook is key to accomplishing great things and persevering through hardship.

As you read, consider how Keller uses:
- *evidence, such as facts or examples, to support claims,*
- *reasoning to develop ideas and to connect claims and evidence, and/or*
- *stylistic or persuasive elements, such as word choice or appeals to emotion, to add power to the ideas expressed.*

Optimism is the faith that leads to achievement; nothing can be done without hope. When our forefathers laid the foundation of the American commonwealths, what nerved them to their task but a vision of a free community? Against the cold, inhospitable sky, across the wilderness white with snow, where lurked the hidden savage, gleamed the bow of promise, toward which they set their faces with the faith that levels mountains, fills up valleys, bridges rivers and carries civilization to the uttermost parts of the earth. Although the pioneers could not build according to the Hebraic ideal they saw, yet they gave the pattern of all that is most enduring in our country to-day. They brought to the wilderness the thinking mind, the printed book, the deep-rooted desire for self-government and the English common law that judges alike the king and the subject, the law on which rests the whole structure of our society.

It is significant that the foundation of that law is optimistic. In Latin countries the court proceeds with a pessimistic bias. The prisoner is held guilty until he is proved innocent. In England and the United States there is an optimistic presumption that the accused is innocent until it is no longer possible to deny his guilt. Under our system, it is said, many criminals are acquitted; but it is surely better so than that many innocent persons should suffer. The pessimist cries, "There is no enduring good in man! The tendency of all things is through perpetual loss to chaos in the end. If there was ever an idea of good in things evil, it was impotent, and the world rushes on to ruin." But behold, the law of the two most sober-minded, practical and law-abiding nations on earth assumes the good in man and demands a proof of the bad.

Optimism is the faith that leads to achievement. The prophets of the world have been of good heart, or their standards would have stood naked in the field without a defender. Tolstoi's strictures lose power because they are pessimistic. If he had seen clearly the faults of America, and still believed in her capacity to overcome them, our people might have felt the stimulation of his censure. But the world turns its back on a hopeless prophet and listens to Emerson who takes into account the best qualities of the nation and attacks only the vices which no one can defend or deny. It listens to the strong man, Lincoln, who in times of doubt, trouble and need does not falter. He sees success afar, and by strenuous hope, by hoping against hope, inspires a nation. Through the night of despair he says, "All is well," and thousands rest in his confidence. When such a man censures, and points to a fault, the nation obeys, and his words sink into the ears of men; but to the lamentations of the habitual Jeremiah the ear grows dull.

Our newspapers should remember this. The press is the pulpit of the modern world, and on the preachers who fill it much depends. If the protest of the press against unrighteous measures is to avail, then for ninety-nine days the word of the preacher should be buoyant and of good cheer, so that on the hundredth day the voice of censure may be a hundred times strong. This was Lincoln's way. He knew the people; he believed in them and rested his faith on the justice and wisdom of the great majority. When in his rough and ready way he said, "You can't fool all the people all the time," he expressed a great principle, the doctrine of faith in human nature.

The prophet is not without honor, save he be a pessimist. The ecstatic prophecies of Isaiah did far more to restore the exiles of Israel to their homes than the lamentations of Jeremiah did to deliver them from the hands of evil-doers.

Write an essay in which you explain how Helen Keller builds an argument to persuade her readers that an optimistic outlook is key to accomplishing great things and persevering through hardship. In your essay, analyze how Keller uses one or more of the features listed above the essay (or features of your own choice) to strengthen the logic and persuasiveness of her argument. Be sure that your analysis focuses on the most relevant features of the passage.

Your essay should not explain whether or not you agree with Keller's argument, but rather explain how Keller builds an argument to persuade her readers.

Practice SAT Essay Passage #3

In this excerpt from his essay "The Philosophy of Sight-Seeing," English journalist and essayist G.K. Chesterton argues that simple touristic sightseeing, though derided by some as vulgar, is in fact a good and worthwhile practice, consistent with how the builders of public monuments meant them to be seen.

As you read, consider how Chesterton uses:
- *evidence, such as facts or examples, to support claims,*
- *reasoning to develop ideas and to connect claims and evidence, and/or*
- *stylistic or persuasive elements, such as word choice or appeals to emotion, to add power to the ideas expressed.*

For the truth is that it has been almost entirely the antiquities that have normally interested the populace; and it has been almost entirely the populace who have systematically preserved the antiquities. The Oldest Inhabitant has always been a clodhopper; I have never heard of his being a gentleman. It is the peasants who preserve all traditions of the sites of battles or the building of churches. It is they who remember, so far as any one remembers, the glimpses of fairies or the graver wonders of saints. In the classes above them the supernatural has been slain by the supercilious. That is a true and tremendous text in Scripture which says that "where there is no vision the people perish." But it is equally true in practice that where there is no people the visions perish.

The idea must be abandoned, then, that this feeling of faint dislike towards popular sight-seeing is due to any inherent incompatibility between the idea of special shrines and trophies and the idea of large masses of ordinary men. On the contrary, these two elements of sanctity and democracy have been specially connected and allied throughout history. The shrines and trophies were often put up by ordinary men. They were always put up for ordinary men. To whatever things the fastidious modern artist may choose to apply his theory of specialist judgment, and an aristocracy of taste, he must necessarily find it difficult really to apply it to such historic and monumental art. Obviously, a public building is meant to impress the public. The most aristocratic tomb is a democratic tomb, because it exists to be seen; the only aristocratic thing is the decaying corpse, not the undecaying marble; and if the man wanted to be thoroughly aristocratic, he should be buried in his own back-garden. The chapel of the most narrow and exclusive sect is universal outside, even if it is limited inside, its walls and windows confront all points of the compass and all quarters of the cosmos. It may be small as a dwelling-place, but it is universal as a monument; if its sectarians had really wished to be private they should have met in a private house. Whenever and wherever we erect a national or municipal hall, pillar, or statue, we are speaking to the crowd like a demagogue.

The statue of every statesman offers itself for election as much as the statesman himself. Every epitaph on a church slab is put up for the mob as much as a placard in a General Election. And if we follow this track of reflection we shall, I think, really find why it is that modern sight-seeing jars on something in us, something that is not a caddish contempt for graves nor an equally caddish contempt for cads. For, after all, there is many a churchyard which consists mostly of dead cads; but that does not make it less sacred or less sad.

The real explanation, I fancy, is this: that these cathedrals and columns of triumph were meant, not for people more cultured and self-conscious than modern tourists, but for people much rougher and more casual. Those leaps of live stone like frozen fountains, were so placed and poised as to catch the eye of ordinary inconsiderate men going about their daily business; and when they are so seen they are never forgotten. The true way of reviving the magic of our great minsters and historic sepulchres is not the one which Ruskin was always recommending. It is not to be more careful of historic buildings. Nay, it is rather to be more careless of them. Buy a bicycle in Maidstone to visit an aunt in Dover, and you will see Canterbury Cathedral as it was built to be seen. Go through London only as the shortest way between Croydon and Hampstead, and the Nelson Column will (for the first time in your life) remind you of Nelson. You will appreciate Hereford Cathedral if you have come for cider, not if you have come for architecture. You will really see the Place Vendome if you have come on business, not if you have come for art. For it was for the simple and laborious generations of men, practical, troubled about many things, that our fathers reared those portents. There is, indeed, another element, not unimportant: the fact that people have gone to cathedrals to pray. But in discussing modern artistic cathedral-lovers, we need not consider this.

Write an essay in which you explain how G.K. Chesterton builds an argument to persuade his readers that sightseeing by tourists is a good practice and not one to be scoffed at. In your essay, analyze how Chesterton uses one or more of the features listed above the essay (or features of your own choice) to strengthen the logic and persuasiveness of his argument. Be sure that your analysis focuses on the most relevant features of the passage.

Your essay should not explain whether or not you agree with Chesterton's argument, but rather explain how Chesterton builds an argument to persuade his readers.

Chapter 13: The Final Word

Well, here we are at the end of *The New SAT Handbook*! We hope that you've found the preceding chapters helpful and instructive. We've covered a lot of ground, including:

- the format of the new SAT test and all its contents

- strategies to read actively and locate what you need in a given passage

- essential principles of grammar and style

- detailed reviews of math concepts and strategies

- the elements of a successful essay

There's also a lot of practice in this book, so if you haven't used it all yet, flip back through Chapters 3, 6, 8, 10, and 12 to brush up on your skills!

And for all the SAT practice you could ever want, remember to visit the College Board's official website: www.collegeboard.org. As the test makers, they have numerous free and accurate resources where you can apply all the skills you've learned here.

Believe it or not, though, there are still a few more things to review before you put this book on your shelf and trot off to ace the SAT.

An important reminder

Your SAT scores will be one component of your college applications, not their end-all-be-all-final-countdown-silver-bullet. Yes, you should try as hard as you can on the SAT—we wouldn't have written this book to help you prepare if that weren't the case—but this test is **_NOT_** a measure of you as a person, or even a full measure of you as a student.

> *It's a measure of how accurately you answer a given set of questions on one weekend morning.*

Just like there will be more to you as a college student than your grades, there will be much more to your college application than your standardized test scores. They are one measure of performance, alongside your high school grades, co-curricular and extracurricular activities, unique talents and abilities, and life experience.

So don't let a college or university's listed "benchmark" or "mid-range" SAT scores hold you back from considering that school. Don't back out of an application because a school requires the Essay Test and you weren't planning on taking it. Don't hesitate to consider a liberal arts program at a larger school even if your Math Test score isn't quite where you wanted it.

In short, don't look at the SAT as a stumbling-block—look at it as one more way to show colleges and universities what you are capable of, *in addition to* everything else you have done. And the better you do on the test, the more of an asset it will be to your application.

That was a lot of "don'ts," so now here is a bunch of "dos" for the SAT—a quick review of all the strategies this book has discussed, along with where to find them.

Reading Test

- *Read the passages actively*. Focus on the whys and hows of each passage.
- Mark up the text and make brief notes as you read. If you're unsure of what to jot down, remember the mnemonic **_NOTE_**:
    - N – Narrative (author's tone, purpose, etc.)
    - O – Opinions (author's, others')
    - T – Thesis (or main idea)
    - E – Evidence (examples, reasoning, etc.)
- When you're answering the questions, ***always go back to the passage***.

Writing and Language Test

- Review the grammar and style concepts discussed in Chapter 5.
- Quickly read the passage, circling any errors you spot on the first pass.
- For each question with an underlined portion:
  - Consider the underlined portion and try to identify the error.
  - Select the answer choice that most effectively corrects the error.
  - If no other answer choice improves on the original, choose A.
- For each question looking at a larger Expression of Ideas concept:
  - Slow down and read the answer choices in the context of the passage.
  - Eliminate answer choices that don't improve upon or add to the passage.
- Overall, for the Writing and Language Test, aim to be ***efficient*** with your time, ***attentive*** to the questions, and ***confident*** in your answer choices

Math Test

- For each question, identify what kind of answer you need and what strategy you want to use to get there.
- Apply the strategies discussed in Chapter 7:
  - ***Straight-Up Textbook***: Apply math concepts the old-fashioned way, using the content you've learned in school. Review the math concepts discussed in Chapter 9 as needed.
  - ***Working the Question***: When working with questions that have answer choices in terms of variables, percents, or ratios, choose a number to use in place of the variable. Solve the question using that number and then plug it into the answer choices to find a match.
  - ***Working the Answers***: When the answer choices are values (usually integers), work backwards strategically by plugging answer choices back into the question to see which checks out. Start with a middle answer choice (**B** or **C**) and if it doesn't work, determine whether you need a bigger or smaller number.
  - ***Working the Test***: When a question has a complicated diagram or graph, or if you're running out of time, use any or all of these three strategies: "Look for a pattern," "Eyeball measurements and draw in additional information," and "Eliminate unreasonable answers."
- Show your work whenever possible to keep track of details and avoid errors.
- Remember that the questions within each section can be answered in any order; skip around and answer the ones you can do fastest first, then go back through and deal with problems that will take more time.

Essay Test

- Read the essay prompt first, then ***actively read the passage*** just like you would in the Reading Test.
- Take a few minutes to ***plan*** your essay before you begin writing; make sure you have a clear thesis statement and evidence to back it up.
- As you write, use paragraphs and transitions to organize your argument.
- Leave a few minutes to ***proofread*** before time is called.
- Avoid Common Essay Problems, discussed in the section beginning on page 228.

If you apply these strategies as you practice for the SAT, then you will definitely feel prepared and confident when you go in to take the real thing! The next section details several things to keep in mind before, during, and after you take the SAT.

Test Day Checklist

Before the test

So you've studied, taken practice tests, and studied some more. You've finally reached the day before the test! How much studying should you do that day?

None.

When you've worked hard to prepare, last-minute cramming will not help you. It will be better for your brain and your confidence if you ***give yourself a break***. Let your mind process and rest.

Do something relaxing: catch an early movie with your friends, go for a jog or a long walk, or enjoy a hobby like video games or crafting. There are only three things you need to do to prepare the day before the test:

1. Pack your bag the night before with everything you'll need for the test so you won't be running around in the morning. (The next section has a list of what to bring and not bring.)
2. Set your alarm so you'll wake up and have plenty of time in the morning.
3. ***Get to bed early!***

The morning of the test, get up and get going! Follow your normal school day routine as closely as possible. Eat a healthy breakfast (nothing too sugary or heavy). Drink what you'd normally drink—it's not the morning to start drinking coffee if you're not a coffee drinker. Grab your things and head out to the test site. Aim to get there early so you'll have time to find your room and get settled in.

Bring/don't bring

Here are the things you should pack and bring with you to the test:

- A photo ID and your test registration ticket
- Sharpened pencils—bring more than you think you'll need—and a sharpener
- Your calculator, with fresh (and spare) batteries
- A water bottle
- Snacks for the breaks
- A sweatshirt in case the room is chilly
- A wristwatch (one that doesn't beep) in case the room doesn't have a clock

These are some things you should leave at home or in the car:

- Your cell phone—if you need it to call your parent, then triple-check that it is turned off before the test, and don't turn it back on until after you've handed in your test booklet!
- This book. Sorry! We wish we could come along with you to cheer you on, but you'll do just great on your own.

During the test

Stay calm and collect your thoughts at the start of each section.

When you know you're almost out of time, double-check your answer booklet to make sure that you've gridded answers properly and filled in anything you omitted. Remember, there's no wrong-answer penalty on the new SAT, so you shouldn't leave anything blank.

Once the proctor calls "time" on that section, it no longer exists! Don't fret about how you did on the previous part of the test; focus on doing your best with just what's in front of you.

Use your breaks wisely. Even if you don't need a water or bathroom break, get up and walk around to get more blood flowing to your brain!

After the test

Congratulate yourself! You did it! You made it through the SAT! If you have the afternoon free, kick back and relax before you have to dive back into your schoolwork and busy life.

Your scores will be available at the College Board website within a few weeks!

Now, before you close this book, please take a moment to do that one thing we asked you to do way back at the beginning of this book.

Tell yourself that you are smart.

Loud and proud, now! "I am smart, and I can handle this test!"

You can handle this test. You've already made a smart decision by planning ahead. Thanks again for choosing this guide to help you prepare!

Good luck!

Index

About the New SAT
Area scores, 11
Composite Score, 11
Subscores, 10
wrong-answer penalty, 11, 111

The Essay Test
About the Essay Test, 3, 9, 10, 96, 217
common essay problems, 228
Expression of Ideas, 42, 43, 45
organization, 220
scoring, 218
Standard English Conventions, 42, 43
thesis statement, 222
tone, 225

The Math Test
About the Math Test, 3, 9, 10, 11, 111-131, 147, 159, 168, 179, 186, 206, 207
Working the Answers, 112, 119, 120, 123, 124, 209
Working the Question, 112, 113-119, 123, 124, 181, 209
Working the Test, 112, 113, 123-129, 209

Arithmetic and Algebra
combination, 157
combining like terms, 148
cross-multiplication, 150, 159
decimals, 162
direct variation, 164
domain, 151
exponents, 186
factoring, 148, 153
factor tree, 154
fractions, 162
function transformations, 166
greatest common factor, 155
imaginary numbers, 204
inverse variation, 164
irregular functions, 165
isolate a variable, 149, 151
least common multiple, 155
linear function, 152
multiples, 153
order of operations, 148
parent functions, 184
percents, 160, 161, 162
polynomials, 177-179, 182-185
primes, 153
proportions, 159
radical expressions, 187
range, 151
rates, 115, 122, 127, 158, 159, 160, 164, 174
rational expressions, 149, 150
rationalize a denominator, 188
reflections, 167
rise over run, 152, 199
slope, 151
slope-intercept form, 152
solve an equation, 149
substitution, 156
system of linear equations, 156
T-chart, 154
translations, 167
y-intercept, 151

Coordinate Geometry
circle in the coordinate plane, 206
distance, 198
distance formula, 199
midpoints, 198
slopes, 198

Data Interpretation
bar graph, 169
circle graph, 168
line graph, 169
sample data, 170
scatterplot, 169
table, 170

Mental Math Drills
    Addition, 132
    Division, 135
    Exponents, 138
    Fractions and Decimals, 136
    Multiples and Factors, 137
    Multiplication, 134
    Subtraction, 133

Plane Geometry
    circles, 197
    congruence, 200
    lines and angles, 189
    polygons, 195
    Pythagorean Theorem, 117, 130, 193, 194, 199
    quadrilaterals, 194
    similarity, 200
    special right triangles, 193
    triangles, 191

Polynomials
    FOIL, 178
    long division, 179
    polynomial expressions, 177
    quadratic, 177
    Quadratic Formula, 183
    special polynomials, 185
    zeros, 182

Statistics
    averages and missing numbers, 175
    Maximum, 172
    Mean, 172
    Median, 172
    Minimum, 172
    Mode, 172
    standard deviation, 175
    weighted averages, 173

Trigonometry
    cosine, 200
    degrees and radians, 205
    sine, 200
    tangent, 200

The Reading Test
About the Reading Test, 3, 9-13, 24, 26, 170
    Analysis of the Topic, 14, 15, 22-25
    Command of Evidence, 14, 15
    inferences, 25
    paired passages, 20
    reading actively, 16
    Vocabulary in Context, 14, 15, 24

The Writing and Language Test
About the Writing and Language Test, 3, 9-11, 41-48, 83, 99, 245

Grammar and Parts of Speech
    adjectives, 48, 63
    adverbs, 48, 63
    antecedent, 71
    article, 48
    auxiliary verb, 79
    clause, 48
    comma splice, 48
    commonly confused pronouns, 72
    comparative, 48, 59
    conjugation, 79
    conjunctions, 48, 53, 76
    continuous tenses, 80
    contraction, 96
    coordination and subordination, 53
    dangling participle, 67
    demonstrative pronoun, 50
    determiner, 48
    diction, 83
    errors of number, 84
    exclamation, 48
    future perfect tense, 51, 80
    gerund, 49, 80
    gerund/infinitive idioms, 84
    fragments, 49, 56
    idioms, 49, 60, 83, 84
    indefinite pronoun, 50
    infinitive, 49
    intensive pronoun, 50
    interjection, 49

interrogative pronoun, 50
modifiers, 49, 63
nouns, 49
noun agreement, 75
object, 49
objective pronoun, 70
parallel structures, 60
parallelism and comparisons, 59
participles, 50, 66, 80, 95
past perfect tense, 51, 80
phrase, 50
possessive pronoun, 71
predicate verb, 50
prepositions, 50
prepositional idioms, 84
present perfect tense, 51, 80
pronouns, 50, 70
reflexive pronoun, 50
relative pronoun, 50
run-ons, 51, 56
sentence, 51
simple future tense, 79
simple past tense, 79
simple present tense, 79
subject, 51
subjective pronoun, 70

subject-verb agreement, 75
subordinating conjunctions, 94
superlative, 51, 59
verbs, 51
verb tenses, 51, 79
word choice, 83

Punctuation
apostrophes, 96
appositives, 90
colons, 91
commas, 89, 90, 93
ellipsis, 98
em dashes, 90
exclamation mark, 88
hyphen, 95
parentheses, 90
periods, 88
question marks, 88
quotation marks, 89
semicolons, 91, 92

Notes

Notes

Notes

Notes

Made in the USA
San Bernardino, CA
06 March 2017